Mutations of Western Christianity

Mutations of
Western Christianity

by ALBERT MIRGELER

Translated by EDWARD QUINN

With a Foreword by DAVID KNOWLES

HERDER AND HERDER

1964

HERDER AND HERDER NEW YORK

232 Madison Avenue, New York 16, N.Y.

This is a translation of Rückblick auf das abendländische
Christentum *(Matthias Grünewald Verlag, Mainz, 1961)*

PRINTED IN GREAT BRITAIN

Foreword

THE historian selects and records events or actions or thoughts of the past, and interprets and presents them. Written history thus consists of facts in the process of becoming thoughts or ideas. The arc of history is wide, stretching from the compilation of annals to the framing of patterns of ideas which rest upon a meagre or even concealed basis of events. The most primitive monastic annals differ from mere lists of names in virtue of the selection of the events which seemed significant to the annalist. Professor Arnold Toynbee's great work, at the other end of the arc, rests upon a framework of reality which distinguishes it from pseudo-historical constructions such as the world-views of Hegel or Marx. Generally speaking, English historians prefer the factual, pragmatic segment of the arc; French historians clarify and order; the Germans, when they are not engaged upon the purely critical investigation of documents, prefer to find and express ideas. Since in this country at the present day German interpretations of history are familiar to very few, Dr Mirgeler's book should be of unusual interest and value.

He is a Church historian, and no class of historian has found the presentation of its subject-matter in terms of ideas so difficult and so perilous. Those who have attempted to do more than give a summary or a narrative of events have often fallen into the biological fallacy that has misled historians of parliament and other institutions. They have presented their theme, whether it was the doctrine of the Real Presence, or the development of the papacy, as one of gradually increasing definition and clarity, from the mists of the early Church to the present time. The present is tacitly regarded as the norm, if not as the ideal, to which the long series of past events is directed. They thus give to the present an element of finality and to the past an element of inevitability. In both past and present the purely historical appearance is lost, for though the present derives its character from the past, the past has seen the action of multifarious agencies, material and spiritual, and it is no part of the historian's task to distinguish between God's design and man's part in failing to accomplish it. We must beware as historians of the slant towards apologetics. Church historians in general say too little about the changes of cultures and of mental climates, and still less about the extravagances, ignorances and misconceptions of sentiment and devotion that have coloured or deformed the purity of the spirit in past centuries and that may well be obscuring for us now in this respect or that the full vision of revealed truth. For there is no reason to suppose that our generation is more spiritually clear-sighted than that of our forefathers, or that the Spirit of truth will not work in the future as He has worked in the past.

Dr Mirgeler has not written a history of the Church. He has not even written an account of the changes of polity and institutions, of the growth and decline of devotions or the elucidation of dogmas. He assumes as well known a background of European history and sketches upon it some of the great changes in the status of Christianity and the racial and sociological influences that have given to the faith and its practice and its institutions a variety of emphasis and outward appearance. The conversion of Constantine, the evangelization of the Germans, the influence of fluid Celtic Christianity, the wrench given to the course of events by the coronation of Charlemagne, the entry of the papacy into world politics in its contest with the empire, with all that

that implied in terms of worldly wisdom and the use of coercive power—all these are seen, not as directly affecting the history of the Church but as transforming the spirit and outlook of generations of Christian people. While he never forgets the divine governance of the Church, and never suggests that the changes he describes imply doctrinal mutability or a total deviation from tradition, he shows that the Church, in its pastors and theologians, as well as in its faithful masses, has been involved in the social and intellectual movements of the world, and has from time to time compromised its own spiritual aims and character, while on the other hand non-religious characteristics and prepossessions have helped to change, and sometimes (as in the development of sacramental confession) to draw out, the manifestations of Christian piety. Though never theologically extravagant, his views are often original, arresting and even provocative.

Opinions of this kind, which are interpretations rather than explanations of the past, may be attractive and may meet with general acceptance, but they are not demonstrably true. The reader who takes them as the "findings of history" would be mistaken, and it would falsify their character to take from them their context and cite them as certain conclusions from clear evidence. But if he uses them to illuminate his own reading and to break down a narrow, formal or tendentious attitude to the past they will enrich his mind and help him towards a penetration in depth of the religious history of Europe.

DAVID KNOWLES

Contents

Contents

I

The Problem

THE question to be discussed in the following pages is that of European Christianity. Strangely enough, it has not been raised explicitly by secular historians: they have been content to note that "Christianity" is undoubtedly a constituent element of "Europe". It was in this sense that Ranke regarded the well-known three factors—Antiquity, Christianity and Germany—as basic to European history. He and still more those who echoed his views were inclined to consider Antiquity and Christianity as pure ideas and therefore in the last resort as supra-temporal factors, endowing European history with a kind of superior justification. Thus it was easy to justify or even simply to take for granted the predominance —to say nothing of the exclusiveness—of Europe in both politics and history over all other parts of the world.

This approach attributed to the third factor—the Germanic peoples—a purely historical and positive character, with a dwindling influence alongside the ideas of Antiquity and Christianity. Consequently, on the one hand, an attempt was made to give to this factor also the force of an idea, a racial or spiritual quality which it did not possess and which therefore could not seriously be compared with the spiritual qualities of Antiquity and Christianity; or, on the other hand, its essential part in the construction of Europe tended to be overlooked.[1]

It may, however, also be asked whether the historical contribution of the other factors is estimated at its true value merely by appealing to the ideas of "Antiquity" and "Christianity". To take these generalizations as absolutes or to assume that everyone knows what they mean, appears to be an over-simplification at a time when there is a tendency to reduce all "essences" to historical reasons, very often going as far as an avowed relativism. In regard to the nature of Christianity it is necessary to look behind the historicism of the nineteenth century and recall that some hundreds of years before this a wide variety of confessional, sectarian and scientific viewpoints had obtained public recognition side by side with one another in Europe.

To raise the historical question of European Christianity is not to deny that the notion of Christianity itself includes also and even primarily a supra-historical element. This supra-historical character is, of course, a matter of faith and not to be grasped by the study of history alone. As far as it is susceptible of a rational explanation, it comes first of all within the scope of theology. It must, however, be admitted on the other hand that Christian theology cannot establish its conclusions regardless of history, since the Christian faith is only possible at all on the basis of a historical revelation. If this holds for Christianity even in its profoundly theological character, then it must be permissible to examine such a complex historical phenomenon as European Christianity also from the standpoint of history.

Naturally, the historical approach—like any other concerned with Christianity—is bound, if not to believe its dogmatic statements, then at least to consider them seriously as a basis of interpretation. But a theological explanation of these statements is not sufficient to account for the role which is generally attributed to Christianity as a main factor in European history and civilization. We are here concerned with a process of commitments going far beyond the field of dogma, taking on innumerable concrete, historical forms of great complexity. In this connection it is not sufficient to note that Europe is, among other things, a creation of "Christianity": we have to ask in all seriousness what kind of

2

a Christianity it was that took shape there. And, since this question has been far too long neglected or has been faced and then set aside as of "mere" historical and not theological interest, it has today a supreme urgency which may well give it priority over what is in itself the more important theological question of the essential nature of Christianity.[2]

For it may well be that this theological question simply cannot be answered satisfactorily today, unless the historical also is introduced and all its implications made clear *in advance*. In an epoch which has discovered in time a fourth dimension of all earthly existence, there is no longer any point in excluding from our considerations any reality as "relative", as if the "absolute" alone were important. The question, therefore, of European Christianity is by no means answered by pointing to the "sacramental nature" of the Church; nor, we might add, is that other favourite question about the future of Christianity. Even if today a narrower, internal problem of the Church must with good reason be answered mainly in the light of this sacramental reality, it must be remembered that the question of European or any other possible Christianity is not purely internal. And indeed it still has to be explained even for the internal, ecclesiastical sphere why—in spite of the zeal of reformers inside and outside of the Church—no one has yet succeeded in presenting this sacramental reality in its "purity" and why, precisely in Europe, it runs the risk of being concealed rather than revealed because of the abundance of its external forms. Just because they are concerned with the "essence" of things, "Reformations" of every kind are eminently historical affairs.

The fact of confessional divisions is not a starting-point for this study : in fact, it will scarcely enter our considerations at all. Essentially, then, we shall be concerned with the Roman Church and pre-Reformation times, though this approach of course cannot fail to throw some light on the Reformation, the Counter-Reformation and the period of the

"Enlightenment". The reason for this limitation of the theme is to be found in the fact that—in my opinion—all the trends of European history were apparent before the Reformation, both in their general character and as affecting our problem in particular.

A new historical situation was created only when in the French Revolution and, above all, in the so-called industrial revolution the consequences of its own history completely transformed Europe. This new datum, anyway, compels us to bring out afresh from the more distant past all the essential questions, including that of European Christianity. That is not to say, however, that this question cannot be handled satisfactorily without an explicit discussion of the present situation. On the contrary, what happened at the Reformation and afterwards can be neither adequately understood nor properly remedied without returning to the medieval scene and its historical presuppositions: that much is evident from the innumerable discussions of theological differences from the time of the Leipzig Disputation[3] onwards. In other words: the settlement of religious differences requires not so much a direct discussion between opposing fronts as an indirect appreciation of historical decisions made long before the Reformation and by which that movement—even when it was opposed to them—never ceased to be governed.

It seems better, therefore, to impose Reformation or post-Reformation standpoints as little as possible on the discussion of these fundamental decisions. Confessional divisions, like most of the spiritual conflicts of history, in spite of their present urgency and insuperability, may one day be seen to be the result of that universal blindness which underlies the historical existence of mankind. As the confessions face each other, they cannot hope to remove this blindness by well-meant attempts to ignore doctrinal differences and to restore a lost unity by returning to points that are not in dispute. It is more likely to be removed by a new basic situation pro-

viding insight into the historical entanglements and consequences which have influenced both sides and are then seen
to be outdated.

This approach to the problem may strike some Catholic
readers as novel and unusual. If they are inclined to be
scandalized and to withdraw to the safe ground of familiar
knowledge—which far too often turns out to be merely
familiar commonplaces—then we may remind them of what
Père de Lubac writes at the end of his book on Catholicism:
"Among Catholics there were not always to be found enough
men living their faith so intensely and so intimately in touch
with the life of their own times as to feel at once particular
difficulties as they arose, and to find, within their own province and on their own responsibility, the required solu-
tions."[4] This fact, which has profoundly affected the development of European Christianity, is nowhere so plainly
evident as in the way in which creative forces were restricted by the defensive attitude imposed on the Church as
a whole in the sixteenth century and on German Catholicism[5] in particular in the nineteenth.

For at first only a very significant part of the real literature of Antiquity was available. In spite of the pompous-sounding names adopted by its members, the so-called Carolingian academy could muster as representative of the ancient world, not Homer or Horace, still less Pindar, Aeschylus or Aristotle, but merely a little Plato and rather more Virgil, together with a misinterpreted Augustine and above all the elementary manuals of Priscian, Boethius and Cassiodorus. It is notorious that these ancient remains were cultivated less for their own sake than as the groundwork of a general education and as an introduction to an appreciation of the liturgy and the Christian writings. Thus, from this standpoint also, Antiquity and Christianity established themselves in reality as an apparently single heritage and in the form acquired in the later age of the Latin Fathers and the imperial Church.

Antiquity as it entered into this combination was, of course, a completely self-sufficient reality; but it only awoke in its true character to new life much later in the two renaissances of the twelfth and the fourteenth to the fifteenth centuries, and then it had to set itself up more or less successfully against the Carolingian amalgam of Antiquity and Christianity. Strictly speaking, therefore, what stands at the beginning of European history is not a triad of Antiquity, Christianity and the Germanic peoples, but two historical powers: the Germanic peoples, who had found precisely in the Frankish empire the form of their historical activity, and the Roman Church which represented the combined heritage of Antiquity and Christianity. The union of these two powers in 751 has always and rightly been regarded as the beginning of a new historical epoch.

The more the Christian element appears at first sight to predominate in this composite heritage, so much the more does the question of its meaning turn out to be not ideological, as it is generally understood, but historical: *what*

8

kind of Christianity was it that brought Europe under its influence?

Christianity had to make its way from the beginning in the form of a "translation". Within the brief span of half a generation, between the death of Christ and the Council of Jerusalem, it had no time to develop a system of life and thought of its own, as Islam did later with its Holy Law.[1] The sacred books of the New Testament themselves appeared after this decisive Council, which sanctioned the Church's mission to the Gentiles, and therefore in this respect are also already included in the theological notion of "tradition".

It would have been difficult anyway to develop such a system of holy law out of the presuppositions of its Jewish origin, for these could have suggested only *one* rational content of Christian faith, namely, the advent of the kingdom of God: that is, since the person of Christ was indispensable to it, the advent of the kingdom through his return. This necessarily eschatological character of the Judaeo-Christian faith held up all attempts to establish a Christian world, as long as that return had not taken place. It was not open to Christianity as it was to Islam to declare the kingdom already present in its fullness and to sum it up in a holy law regulating every aspect of life: for at its centre stood the person of Christ, not the eternal book of the Koran merely revealed afresh to Mohammed. The delay of the *Parousia*—which still continues today—would have left a purely Jewish Christianity—that is, the primitive Christianity so often presented as the ideal—in a state of great embarrassment and from any merely human standpoint would probably have meant its slow decline, such as in fact did occur in the Jewish-Christian group.

The fact that Christianity, right at the beginning, shook off the soil of its origin appears therefore to have been the very condition of its historical existence. The comparison with Islam shows that this historicity is essential to it, not merely "accidental". It is impossible for Christianity to have a holy law of the kingdom, like that of Islam; and, of course, for that reason it has been protected from Islam's fate of falling into the historical sterility resulting from the immutability of such a divine law. Moreover, there remains *also* as the root of the historical character of Christianity the fact that it is directed towards a final kingdom, the kingdom proclaimed by Christ. It lasts only as long as the kingdom is still in the future—in theological terms, as long as Christ's return is delayed.

Christianity is thus compelled to regard itself as a historical reality, as in a state of transition between its Jewish past and the eschatological future of the kingdom of God. Paul developed such a conception in his epistles; but this was a purely theological self-awareness, no longer adequate when Christianity had taken a decisive turning by passing from Jerusalem to Rome.

The problem consisted in the fact that Judaism presented for the polity united under Roman rule anything but a normal tradition : it seemed rather something to be abhorred by mankind. The question was therefore inevitably bound to arise as to how a revelation emerging out of Jewish history could claim universal importance. We cannot deny that, from the standpoint of the ancient world, nothing was more natural than the attempt of Marcion and the Gnostics to throw aside Christianity's Jewish past and embody it in a universality of a mythical character which was already at hand and had always been there. Early Christianity decisively rejected this attempt to reduce it to a common level, firmly upheld the Old Testament as its pre-history and brought to completion the historico-juridical order of its Church. But it thereby became all the more urgent to justify and make credible this self-assertion, to explain why a Church emerging out of Jewish history and Jewish forms of worship could be of importance to all mankind and its missionary preaching universally binding. It was decisive for the Church that she had to call to her aid in this task the resources of the old antagonist of mythology, the philosophy of the ancient world.

From the historical standpoint, the Church was merely a particular phenomenon, one of the many *religiones* competing for the soul of Rome. As a separatist movement from the Jewish national and religious community, it had to make itself known from the beginning more as a cult than as a people, although the sense of being the true Israel—the people of God of the New Testament—belonged to its essential content. This ethnic element might be called the lay-consciousness of the Church, the term being derived from the Greek λαός. But this was inevitably overshadowed by a "clerical" consciousness, which was to a greater degree a formative element in the Church; for the Church's members were not united as a race as the Jews had been, but took on the form merely of a secession of individual converts and gained any sense they had of being a united people solely in the act of worship taking place in their presence under the leadership of the clergy.

In times of persecution, of course, the common act of worship became at least more difficult and the witness of the individual gained a correspondingly greater importance: for a time there might have been the possibility of a Church in which personal witness was fundamental, which therefore could have developed into a group of sectarian witnessing communities. In the third and fourth centuries this possibility was finally excluded as a result of the controversies about re-admission of the lapsed and the Donatist schism: the Church ultimately emerged as a centre of worship and as an official institution.* What concerns us here is the fact

* *Kultkirche* and *Amtskirche*, to be translated henceforward as "worshipping Church" and "institutional Church" (Tr.).

that such witnessing communities would have been historical oddities, to an even greater degree than the worshipping Church: for this had in its supra-personal basis a greater assurance of historical permanence.

In spite of its Jewish origin, this worshipping Church made its way among the pagans. Precisely because of the success of its mission, the question arose as to how Judaism—which, as a result of the acceptance of the Old Testament as canonical, remained an integral part of Christianity—and how a worshipping Christian church cut off from this could go beyond it to claim meaning and validity for all mankind. In the answer to this question was involved the assertion—which, in view of the level of education attained in Antiquity, had to be maintained—that only a *rationale obsequium* and not any arbitrarily chosen religious activity could be binding on men. It involved also the credibility of the claim to appeal to all men: in other words, the character of Christianity as a world-religion.[2]

The answer to the question required an appeal to the universal ($\varkappa\alpha\theta'\,\delta\lambda o\upsilon$), understood both in the rational and in the social sense. That is why "catholic" is one of the indispensable and essential attributes of the Church. It is important to note that this predicate must not be understood in a purely theological sense, but that the appeal to the universal in human reason and social instincts calls and embodies into the scheme what may be regarded as "natural" aspects of existence—philosophy and history.[3]

We might now have been expected to answer the question of the universality of Christianity by pointing to its historical incorporation into the development of humanity. This has in fact been done to some extent even in the field of theology, through the scheme developed there of Creation, Fall and Redemption. But it was a scheme which had to be restricted to the theological field, because of the absence of a full awareness of history and therefore also of a doctrine of the structure of universal history; it was thus unable to include the much more extensive field of secular history.

From this last point of view the theological epochs of the Creation and the Fall reach back into a mythical pre-history, beyond the scope of research, while, on the other hand, revelation is concentrated on the Jewish people and the Christian Church, that is, on unique and comparatively small sections of the whole process of world-history. We must not forget of course that the Old Testament also in the first eleven chapters of Genesis set revelation against the background of universal history; but, because of the absence of historical insight into the whole scheme, the theological line of development from the Jewish people to the Christian Church remained for a long time not merely typical but almost the sole determining factor of historical awareness.

Apart from this, notice was taken only of sporadic traditions belonging to a particular field of history and these, as soon as the time became ripe, were linked up with awareness of the Church to form a Christian universal history. A familiar example of this process is our Christian way of reckoning time (introduced, strangely enough, for pre-Christian times only at the period of the Enlightenment): Christ is set up as the turning point of time, but this is a purely theological approach, useless to secular history. For secular history today no longer works with particular reckonings of time—such as the Roman, *ab urbe condita*, or the Islamic, from the *hegira* onwards—but with completely different divisions of epochs, about which there is not and need not yet be complete unanimity.

The reason for this failure to establish a basis in human history for the universal validity of Christianity lies in the fact that in the ancient world, in which Christianity was faced with this problem of self-justification, reason had developed only a purely philosophical and not yet an historical self-awareness. Universal history became a theme for rational discussion only from the ages of the Enlightenment and of Romanticism, and the inquiry is still being keenly pursued.

In early Christian times, Irenaeus was able to work out only the abstract idea of a progressive education of the human race, out of which emerged the temporal succession of natural, mosaic and evangelical law. But for the pagan world it was a question of the possibility of a direct transition to Christianity, by-passing historical Judaism. That is why the question of the universal significance of Christianity —that is, of the catholicity of the Church—could not up to the present time be given a genuinely historical answer: which is as much as to say that it could not properly be answered at all.

The question could be faced only on the purely philosophical level: a level at which formal statements alone are permissible; if concrete assertions are required, historical data must be brought in. If, without the aid of these, "abstract" philosophy illegitimately oversteps its competence and draws concrete conclusions—as has frequently happened in the field of European history—then one of two mishaps occurs. Sometimes historical data of this kind are tacitly assumed and then concrete conclusions can be valid within the scope of these data. That is what happened, for instance, with the demonstration of Christian Europe: in the last resort, with the aid of Roman Law and Aristotelian philosophy, it succeeded only in proving its origin from Antiquity and thus no more than the fact of its own existence. On the other hand, philosophy may exceed its authority and replace the complexity and variability of the concrete by formal, abstract concepts and try to impose these on reality with the uniformity of the universal transformed into a merely factual individuality. That is the way of all the "isms" and ideologies which led in the course of European history to attempts to realize the kingdom: attempts made in good faith and not intentionally destructive, but leading in practice—as Hegel saw[4]—to what in modern times we have come to describe as "terror".

Thus, from the beginning, there was implicit in the association of Christianity with a philosophy lacking historical foundation and formation the dual fate of terror and secularization: terror, in so far as Christianity tried to impose its "ideas" with the aid of political power; secularization, in so far as it was pressed into service for the ideological interpretation of mundane affairs by the philosophy and political power with which it was allied.

III

The Alliance with Philosophy

AT the time when Christianity had to commend itself to the Roman world, Stoicism was still the popular and dominant philosophy. The reason for its extraordinary impact lay in the simplicity of its principles on the one hand and in its concentration on moral responsibility on the other. Stoicism regarded the cosmos as a work of art, deliberately shaped and upheld by a creative *logos*: man had a share in the *logos* and therefore a foremost place in the scheme, and—as a result of his free-will—a special task to fulfil. This last was the reason for his moral duty of strict self-discipline and the maintenance of an absolute dominion of the *logos* over the passions and the feelings, a task which became of the greatest importance at the time of the late Roman Empire and the beginning of Christianity.

To those for whom political life had lost all meaning when they became subjects of the Roman Empire (as also at an earlier stage to those of the great hellenistic states) Stoicism thus offered a new fulcrum: the ideal of inward repose (ataraxy), rendering them immune from the adversities and unpleasantness of their passive and servile existence. On the other hand, it could offer to rulers also a moral support and thus become the official philosophy of the Roman Empire, as a visible embodiment of the divine law of the cosmos, and an ideal of character for its emperors and officials.

Moreover, Stoicism made it possible for emperors, their officials and their intellectually fastidious subjects both to adopt a rational attitude and to share the official belief of the State and thus of the Roman people or even—as the emperor did when acting as *pontifex maximus*—to take the lead in these. This was possible on the basis of the theology of history developed by Panaetius in the second century before Christ: the theory of a succession of mythological, political and philosophical religions (*theologia tripertita*).[1] To the last of these, according to Panaetius' disciple, Porphyry, there fell the supreme task of restoring the pure idea of God held by mankind at its origin, in the "Golden Age", when it shared in the primeval divine power. Just as Islam later recognized Judaism and Christianity as preparatory stages, so the Stoic in the light of this theology could also recognize the mythological and the political faiths as preparatory—though unpurified—stages of his own philosophical religion and might even take part in their observances.

In the second century, Christianity saw its belief in God the Creator threatened by the Gnostic movements with their doctrines of the senselessness of earthly existence and of an evil world-creator. Against this devaluation of the world the Stoic philosophy, with its doctrine of a rational cosmos wholly under the theological ordering of providence, could not but be a welcome aid. Their meeting was brought about deliberately, as a result of the Christian conviction that everywhere and therefore also among the pagans there had been sown the seed of truth (λόγος σπερματικός). Christian philosophy actually began with Clement of Alexandria in the form of an attempt simply to christianize Stoicism, which was taken over as a preparatory study to Christianity.

From then onwards, the Fathers of the Church were "never tired of pointing out that all the paradoxical characteristics attributed to the Stoic sages really belong to the perfect Christian who is pleasing to God".[2] Seneca and Cicero became authorities for Roman and therefore also for Western Christianity—in fact, as the legend of Seneca's secret conversion shows, almost Christians *avant la lettre*. Although this close amalgamation later broke down, there were still two motives above all which justified a permanent association of Stoic ideas with Christianity : they were valid at that time as they were at the renaissance of Stoicism—the importance of which has been brought out at length by Dilthey —during the transition from the Confessional age to the age of reason in the seventeenth century.

In the first place, when Christianity as a result of the delay of the *Parousia* had to face the prospect of permanent existence on this earth, the Stoic idea of a universal divine law provided a philosophical expression also of its relationship to the secular aspects of life (and not merely to the eschatological future). So-called "Natural Law" placed even worldly activity under a divine rule; on the Christian side, it was identified with the Mosaic law and therefore seemed to contain standards by which contrary regulations and dispositions of positive law might be judged.

In the second place, the moral pathos of Stoicism emphasized—particularly at a time of political and moral upheaval —the value of the human person as a rational being and made him the centre of a regeneration to be effected by rising above "passion", first of all in private life and then in public affairs. This moral pathos certainly led to exclusiveness, isolating too much the activity of the human will and at least underestimating the importance of the body and the emotions: Epictetus, for instance, held that the body was one of those external things which "do not concern us".[3] In questions of natural law also a survey of the actual situation inevitably took second place, while the moral or at any rate teleological standpoint predominated; that is why, even in modern times, great efforts have had to be made to elaborate against this background the factual structures of natural science, biology and history.

Two further parallels between the Stoic and the Christian attitudes must be mentioned, which indicate how the earlier Stoic formulation affected the development of Christianity.

In contrast to Stoicism, primitive Christianity had indeed firmly rejected any participation in the pagan cult of nation and State, not even hesitating to confirm this hostility if necessary by martyrdom. Nevertheless, the Stoic theology of history was able to influence the Christian outlook to the extent of creating a desire to gain a deeper understanding of those truths of faith which concerned the mass of Christians "only" from the point of view of worship. This distinction became important beyond the inevitably small circle of genuine philosophers when the youthful Germanic peoples entered into the role of Christian believers.

Not having the previous experience of the ancient world or a knowledge of the Latin language, a deeper understanding of Christianity was bound to escape them and even the liturgy inevitably to remain more or less alien. For them the Christian lay-consciousness as the people of God was switched over to the political plane—as the chosen people of the Franks—or to the moral. In this situation it became, so to speak, an *arcanum imperii* of the ecclesiastical hierarchy to reserve to its own circle the liturgy, still more theology properly so-called, and even to a large extent mystical experience. Mystical impulses on the part of the laity were taken over as far as possible in the form of religious communities and the communities of men clericalized by ordination. In this way two levels of Christian life were established and remained clearly distinct up to the beginning of the present century: even the reading of the Bible was reserved to priests and monks, while the laity were in practice restricted to obligatory participation in a minimum of liturgy, to morality and a varied and exuberant popular piety.

The second important factor was the Stoic view of the universal in human reason and ethics as constituting the *genus humanum*, that is, humanity in its positive biological status. Reason is indeed given as an endowment to all men, but it is only properly effective after suitable training and then in very different forms. The Stoics had forgotten Aristotle's observation that, "though sense-perception is innate in all animals, in some the sense-impression comes to persist, in others it does not", and that "a further distinction arises between those which out of the persistence of such sense-impressions develop a power of systematizing them and those which do not".[4] They forgot therefore the more important aspect of their philosophical heritage: namely, that reason means for man not so much a necessary endowment as a practical vocation which he can or will fulfil only in varying degrees.

The Stoic *logos* thus became marked with an ambiguity which even today is not fully cleared up: it is in fact an attribute of anything which bears the human shape and, on the other hand, a norm transcending positive existence. Reason then—and, of course, the transcendent equality of men before God which it implied—was liable to become confused with the biological-sociological destiny of humanity. This misunderstanding became easier when, after the christianization of the Roman Empire, all citizens became by that very fact also Christians. But it became fatal only when this universal Christianity turned in modern times into that secularized reason which interpreted all the Christian facts in a human way and thus became the common source of both the Enlightenment and the German Idealism which reacted against it.

It then became possible to regard all men as such not only as rational, but also as Christian: even to consider pagans as "better" men and, in fact, as Christians. On the other hand, as a result of equating humanity, reason and possibly Christianity, all distinctions were abolished and all men and all Christians had to be considered as "by nature" equal; any differentiation within this equality appeared to be trivial, if not positively wrong. Hence in modern times, one consequence of the Stoic theory of natural law could become dominant which appeared only spasmodically and without permanent success in Antiquity: the phenomenon of revolution. As a result above all of the French Revolution, the principle of the natural equality of men has become established in the laws of states and in international law and has created a world in which the Church's distinctions between priests, religious and laity, and even between the dead as blessed, suffering or damned, emerge as odd relics from a distant past now become unintelligible and incredible.

With the aid of Stoic philosophy Christianity was able to defend the fact of a rational world, created by a "good" God, against Gnosticism. But this alliance had quite clearly defined limits, for the Stoic God was a principle immanent in the world and in some sense material. Against this pantheistic-materialist immanence Christianity had to assert the transcendence of a God superior to the world, who created it out of "nothing". The transcendental tendencies of the time helped in the fulfilment of this task, finding their expression in an abundance of religious cults, but also slowly replacing the hitherto dominant Stoicism by a renewal of Platonism. This Neo-Platonism underlined the notion of a transcendent God, which had been established by Plato and Aristotle; thus it seemed to offer in the long run a more suitable conceptual basis for Christianity than did Stoicism, irremediably arrested in the teleological notion of the cosmos. And yet here also concrete difficulties arose as a result of the fact that there lay behind the concepts of Platonism the same "technomorphous" pattern[5] as that behind Stoicism: it was difficult to advance from this conceptual basis to the idea of creation out of nothing and equally difficult to rise to the thought of personality in the supreme being.

"If we look for the primary phenomenon from which Idealism arises, it is clearly to be seen everywhere in Plato's works. It is always manual and artistic creation to which

21

Plato turns and from which he draws his examples. Whether the carpenter constructs a loom or the architect builds a house, they always work in the light of a plan, of an 'idea', and they have before them the material to which they give form and shape corresponding to a mental exemplar. The creator of the world himself in Plato becomes in the last resort a 'demiurge', a craftsman who looks to the realm of ideas as to a mental world-plan and then constructs the corporeal world in space and gives it material shape."[6] In passing, it may be said that the whole of Europe's later development towards a "perfect technique" and an "art for art's sake" is implied in this sort of approach. Aristotle developed it into a conceptual apparatus rich enough to put in the shade all that had gone before and adopted it for almost every sphere of knowledge, even in those which this key did not fit at all.[7]

The dialectic of such a philosophy meant that in practice the production of both the craftsman and the artist remained in the grip of philistinism. The really well-bred Greek had to occupy himself with better things than handling material and therefore turned to inter-personal activities: politics and —after Plato had shown how these had degenerated—philosophy. But here the social basis, "philosophizing with one another", was soon lost precisely as a result of this conception of philosophy as a kind of production. It became a solitary activity, akin to the handling of material, though its material was rarefied into ideas and essences. Aristotle regarded the "theoretic life" as the highest possible share in the divine open to man, a life going beyond both the social and productive spheres which had provided its conceptual basis.

This dialectic also had metaphysical consequences. It was important, for instance, to separate the creator of the world (demiurge) from the supreme God and subordinate him to the latter. Plato and Plotinus drew these conclusions, each in his own fashion, as also did the Arian Aetius in a Christian setting.[8] And out of a philosophy centred on "ideas" or "essences" there arose a theology of the neuters—*ens, unum, verum, bonum*, etc.[9]—as with Plato it had also culminated in the "idea of the good", which could only be expressed as neuter.

Plato and Aristotle did indeed advance in this way to a notion of God, in the purity of which they could well take pride when they compared it to the fables of the poets and mythologists. But on closer examination it could be seen that this God was not a personal first mover, as he came to be understood and seemed to be in retrospect from the Christian point of view, but the first moving reality.[10] Such a notion—as the Arabian philosophers were to observe—was quite compatible with the basic Aristotelian axiom of the eternity of the world,[11] as also with the later Stoic view of a God without feelings or passions;[12] but it was harder to reconcile with the Christian axioms of three persons in God and of God's personal relationship to men. It needed a great effort before the juridical and dogmatic concept of person found its way into Christian philosophy, with Leontius of Byzantium (475-543); and it was only with medieval scholasticism that this event gained greater importance in Europe.[13]

Neo-Platonism, perhaps even more than Stoicism, blocked the way to an appreciation of historical realities. Reality was attributed solely to the supra-mundane "One", from which by a process of emanation all other realities were derived; these must therefore be regarded as lesser beings, although of the same quality as the One. When the concrete as such had thus been deprived of meaning, the allegorical method came into play and had considerable success also in Christianity, leading to a conception of the world which could be understood only in Christian terms.

This occurred on a large scale, however, only when the

C   23

genuine Christian motives for allegorizing—the attempt to explain transcendent truth in the manifold of its earthly aspects—faded out more and more after the migration of the peoples. At that time the younger nations, accessible to symbolic thought, began to shape their own destinies and the rational Roman Law ceased simultaneously to form the universal basis of social existence. Symbolic thinking must in fact be taken generally as a midway stage between the group-thought of the tribe and rational reflection on the world as a whole; it represents the beginning of an appreciation of spiritual data, but in such a way that these are still seen as embodied in visible things.

It is interesting to note that figures like Charlemagne and Agobard of Lyons, who were still so familiar with the ancient outlook, did not indulge in symbolism, while almost simultaneously Amalarius of Metz and Rabanus Maurus were securing its triumph for the Middle Ages. In this they went far beyond the allegorizing method inherited from Neo-Platonism—or perhaps it would be more correct to say that they adopted a far less rational approach. While the Neo-Platonists started out from the rational "One", finding its traces in concrete reality, the medieval symbolists started out in the opposite direction from the concrete thing, but turned their attention away from this at once, not towards the rational "One", but to an "Other" revealing itself to them in the concrete thing. In this way they mostly came across concrete features which the concrete reality had in common with other things. Thus from different points of view there could be seen under the veil of the same concrete reality a multiplicity and variety of "Others": in the lion, for example, there appeared the sovereign Lord and bloodthirsty beast of prey, Christ, "the lion of Juda", as well as the devil who "goes about, roaring like a lion". At the end we find that world of late medieval symbolism which Huizinga described in his *Waning of the Middle Ages*[14]: multicoloured, wholly enchanted, a world in which each thing might mean almost anything except itself and in which every quality might be personified. This end was not reached as a result of a false turning, but through the logical application of a principle which already for Rabanus Maurus represented the key to the whole world of sense.[15]

This form of allegorizing became vitally important in the history of the Western Church, particularly because of its grip on the central forms of Christian tradition: the Bible and the liturgy. From the time of Amalarius and Rabanus deeper meanings were supposed to be concealed behind every word of the Bible and every liturgical act.

The possibility of multiplying such interpretations meant that any appreciation of the concrete situations and statements in the Bible, as well as the interconnection of the whole, was lost. The Bible could be used—as Augustine showed—as a kind of oracle for practical decisions, but also on the other hand as a proof of any and every theory: the medieval doctrine of the two swords, for instance, was based on the text of Luke 22.38, torn completely out of its context ("See, Lord, they told him, here are two swords. And he said to them, That is enough"). But the importance to the masses of this allegorical interpretation should not be exaggerated. It was the Reformation which first made the Bible more widely accessible, but even then in Protestant areas alone; on Catholics—apart from the readings in church-services—it had only an indirect impact, through the preaching of priests and monks to whom it was *ex officio* entrusted.

A more important influence was the allegorical interpretation of the Mass, which reached the Franks from the East and through the works of the Pseudo-Dionysius.[16] It became more or less necessary when Latin had become a foreign language and a meaning at least perceptible to sense had to be found in the otherwise unintelligible liturgical acts.[17] This of course, like any allegorical meaning, could be multiple;

but the general trend until long after the Spanish *autos sacramentales* (among them, holding first place, Calderon's *Mysteries of the Mass*) was to interpret the Mass as a pictorial presentation of the life and sufferings of Christ.

The persistence of this allegorical explanation right up to our own times is so much more astonishing in that it was condemned as early as 838 by the Synod of Quiercy as an affront to the *rationale obsequium* required of us; it was also rejected at the opening of the great age of Scholasticism by Albert the Great as "nonsense and the work of uneducated men (*deliramenta et hominum illiteratorum*)". At this point even the rational approach of Scholasticism remained ineffective and powerless. The ancient Christian celebration of the common sacrifice and sacrificial meal, in which the people also have part, is thus a purely objective act, "the Eucharist has become the epiphany".[18] All that interested the people in the Mass was the sacramental presence, which remained also outside the Mass and was at their disposal apart from this; this aspect was emphasized from about 1200 onwards by the elevation of the Host. In the sacramental presence the "reality" of the symbolism was assured, since in the last resort under the forms of bread and wine the full reality of what is symbolized is available.

IV

Politics

THE meeting of Christianity with philosophy was its first and, in effect, decisive meeting with the world. The importance of this became clear only at a very late stage, although its consequences for European history were far-reaching. We have seen that the full acceptance of ancient thought by scholastic philosophy had no noticeable effect at all in so important a field as that of liturgy; later, under the pressure of the uncompromising religious thought of Reformation times, Luther was sometimes brought to the verge of revoking this acceptance in principle. It was only after the upheaval of the Enlightenment that thought set itself up as sovereign and claimed total dominion. In relation to Christianity it now stood for the indispensability of a *rationale obsequium*, that is, for the rational presuppositions which had already been recognized in principle in the late Roman and scholastic meeting with philosophy. Furthermore, although this philosophy remained unaware of historical problems, its revolutionary and equalitarian consequences now began to make themselves felt: philosophy turned to the attack, not only on historical Christianity, but also on the power which had hitherto provided the framework of life: the State.

Events such as the meeting of Christianity with the world or the awakening of man's philosophical consciousness, in spite of their extraordinary importance, cannot be considered historically merely for their own sake and in their own setting. It is more important to see them against the general background of a world-shaping force which was dominant in the great ages of history from the foundation of the states in the river-valleys of the Nile and of Mesopotamia to Napoleon and—as an anachronism—even up to our own times: the background of politics.

Man's philosophical consciousness, which has been slowly covering over this background from the age of Enlightenment, was of course also able to look back to a long period of incubation before then. Plato had in fact raised the demand that philosophers should become kings and kings philosophers, but philosophical politics and even political philosophy exercised at the most an indirect, never a really determining influence on political life. Even the first contacts of Christianity with philosophy took place against the political background of the Roman Empire, and it was this background which at once appeared as the determining influence on Christianity when the Empire entered into a positive association with it. Thus for Christianity as such the alliance with philosophy came first, but for Western Christianity the alliance with politics was more decisive.

This alliance, as is well known, was set up by Constantine the Great, the first Roman Emperor to become a Christian—though baptized only on his death-bed. In view of the consequences of this event for the later history of Christianity, we can speak of it as the "Constantinian turning-point". There can scarcely be a more obvious sign of the ending of an epoch than the opposition which that alliance rouses today not only among non-Christians, but also among Christians of all shades of belief.

In spite of this new situation, we must be careful not to commit ourselves to the current impression that the Constantinian turning-point "perverted" Christianity. This is a way of speaking which usually starts out from the belief that Christianity was free to come to terms with the world or not, and that the mere abandonment of the political ties accepted under Constantine would have led to a "pure" or at least purer Christianity. In such a theory the Incarnation is either not taken seriously at all or so toned down that it becomes a unique event at one point of time, without any genuinely historical consequences; its traces would be left merely in individual souls or at most in a series of positive doctrines or means of salvation.

The biblical view is very different: it does not take the Incarnation simply as an isolated and unique event or as an historical accident, but places it in a meaningful context with the whole sequence of Old Testament events and thus also with the whole of history—since the Old Testament begins not only at Sinai, but at the creation of the world. And if from the theological standpoint the event of the Incarnation has its significant historical situation in the "fullness of time", then the Christianity derived from it has a necessary relationship to history and at any particular time its own place in the historical sequence. In an age which—rightly or wrongly —has been formed and shaped by political power, Christianity also has to take on a primarily political character in its relations with the world. The Constantinian turning-point inaugurates the Christianity appropriate to an era in which— to adopt Napoleon's dictum—politics is destiny.

It is of course very doubtful whether this judgment was valid even for Napoleon's own time, still more whether it can hold for ours; but there can be no doubt at all that it was true of the time of Constantine and for long afterwards. To demand for that age an unpolitical, still more a purely spiritual Christianity, would mean asking for a Christianity aloof from the destiny of its time and which consequently would itself have been left behind by that destiny. The only solution at the time was the Constantinian. Abelard in his day maliciously observed that the success of Christianity before it received the massive support of the Emperors had been very slight.[1] It is in fact also our opinion that a continuance of the age of the martyrs—naturally, purely imaginary—or even the orientation of Christian practice towards that age, as the Donatists suggested, would sooner or later have reduced Christianity to an insignificant sect so that by our time it would—humanly speaking—have ceased to exist. The decisive historical counter-test, which shows how right was the Constantinian move, was made by Islam : in Muslim countries Christianity is in fact one of the tolerated religions, but today is practically extinct. And it is clear from missionary work outside Europe that even quite considerable success is of no avail as soon as a decisive political opposition sets in.

If the Christian alliance with politics is regarded today with a critical eye, this seems to me to be merely a result of the new world-situation in which politics itself can no longer escape effective philosophical criticism. In this situation it is particularly important to note the weighty historical consequences which emerged for Christianity after the Constantinian turning-point and which perhaps were suitable only under the conditions of the time. Incidentally, we must note that generalizations about the "corruption" of Christianity by politics only lead us to neglect this task instead of taking it in hand. It was not taken in hand in the nineteenth century and Catholicism, with its political and social status undermined after the French Revolution, aimed mainly at the restoration and regaining of the old positions, taking the form of "political" and "social Catholicism" : all this turns out today to be a severe handicap to any attempts at a convincing fresh start. Today, in the conditions of a new age, we have to examine afresh the Constantinian turning-point both in itself and in all its consequences.

We have now to consider a number of important changes which Christianity underwent as a result of the Constantinian turning-point. It is obvious, but needs again to be emphasized, that we are primarily concerned with historical developments. From the theological standpoint there can naturally only be a shift of emphasis within a given dogmatic scheme. But we must not regard such shifts of emphasis as negligible or think that they become irrelevant as soon as we concentrate solely on the "sacramental nature" of the Church. On the contrary, they are at every point decisive for the historical reality of the Church and of Christianity: we have already seen that the divergence between the historical shape and its dogmatic foundations can go very far, under certain circumstances indeed so far as to leave dogmatic principles merely an obscure existence in theological treatises unknown to the general public.

1. For the Romans, even more than for other peoples who have shaped the course of history since the State began, religion was an integral part of public law: "religion" meant the sum-total of official acts of worship and the beliefs lying behind these. This sphere became more restricted in the course of time but was not thereby affected in its nature, since in the later Empire what remained binding and obligatory on all subjects was practically only the dual requirement of taking part in Emperor-worship, and of regarding the Emperor as divine lord (*dominus*, κύριος).

Christianity had opposed this demand, invoking Christ as Lord and worshipping him as God, but in a concrete form similar to that of the reverence paid to the Emperor—with incense and lights carried before him. In all this, of course, the fact recognized from the beginning was kept in mind: that this God had become man and in the Eucharist had extended his union with human nature to all the "faithful". Christians, therefore, formed that part of humanity which was conscious of a supra-mundane destiny with all its consequences and which made earthly life into a quest—so to speak—of complete union with the God who had become man.

The Christian faith, then, could never completely with-

31

draw as it were into its own self-sufficiency, in the form of a mere "religion" apart from the rest of life. Dogma was not just a series of "articles of faith" to be grasped objectively, but included inevitably also a statement about the present location both of Christians and of all humanity. Thus in the creed the location of the Christian is seen to be the Church (*credo ecclesiam*, without the *in*, while at the beginning we have *credo in Deum*), the location of all humanity the end of time—that is, the last age before the Second Coming. The Church directs her steps towards the returning Christ: this existential situation found striking expression in the Roman "Station Mass", in which the "procession" led to the Christ of the Eucharistic sacrifice.

This historical emphasis was lost when the Roman emperors adopted Christianity. Christianity then began to be regarded as essentially a State religion and a State cult. Both of these tended to become self-sufficient in a sphere of their own remote from ordinary life, a sort of anticipation of a future beyond this world and thus already a fulfilment of the eschatological expectation. People no longer thought of "secular" life as a way leading to another world. The liturgical procession, consequently, was reduced to the Introit; and this, in turn, as it lost its processional character, became merely the opening of the act of worship.[2] Within the scheme of the Christian empire the world itself ceased to be an event and became a static reflection of heaven: medieval symbolism regarded as its main task the understanding and representation of this in the light of the teaching of Dionysius the Areopagite.

2. As soon as Christianity had gone beyond its Constantinian status as a *religio licita* (State-tolerated religion) to become under Theodosius the exclusive State religion, *all* citizens necessarily and under pain of legal sanctions became Christians. The equivalence of "man" and "Christian" was established by the State, regardless of the fact that the poli-

tical necessity of such a common cult—normal as it was in all the ancient kingdoms—was unknown to the Gospels; on the contrary, the appropriation of the good tidings appeared there as expressly the concern of the "few", who, moreover, had before them the prospect of going as sheep among wolves.[3] To the identity of "man" and "Christian" in the Empire there corresponded then the identification of non-Christian with political enemy : thus it became easy to justify the imperial claim to carry out missionary activity by war-like acts and measures of force, a claim exemplified later in the action of Charlemagne against the Saxons.

It is interesting to note that a form of Christianity for the few—monasticism—appeared almost simultaneously with the Constantinian turning-point. But the basis had essentially changed. For if previously it had been a question simply of a small number of Christians in a world of non-Christians, it was now a matter of an *élite* in a world that had become Christian. When these were confronted with one another, the Christianity of the majority almost inevitably appeared as one of lower standards, not as having a proper level in virtue of its essential nature. Monasticism ran the risk of having to justify its character as an *élite* less from the transcendent-historical situation of the Christian way (the "procession") than from the ascetic standpoint of its outstanding moral achievement.

3. Since the Roman Empire as the cultural sphere of the οἰκουμένη was distinguished from the human beings outside the State as from the *barbarae nationes*, when it became Christian, the way was open to an identification both of Christianity and culture and—on the other hand—of paganism and barbarism. In the Middle Ages this identification had a great deal to do with the estrangement and final division between the Greek and the Western Church. Since to the assumption of cultural superiority there was added the Christian sense of being an elect—a sense that had hitherto

belonged only to the Church as the new Israel—the Empire
could not but conceive itself as the representative of a "Christian culture" in the midst of an otherwise barbarian world;
the authentic Christian experience of being a minority among
the non-Christians of the immediate environment had been
transferred to the sphere of politics and geography. Thus the
notion of the "catholicity" of the Church was reduced to
that of geographical extension by incorporation into the
Empire and later by the formation of new Christian states. It
is significant that a properly ecclesiastical missionary centre
appeared only in 1622 when the *Congregatio de propaganda
fide* was set up.

4. In virtue of the equation of Empire and Church
(*imperium-ecclesia*), the Emperor became the decisive figure
also in the Church: it was the Emperor's Church. Constantine had already given himself the title of "Christ's representative" (*vicarius Christi*) and arranged for his body to be
buried in the Church of the Apostles in the midst of those of
the twelve apostles which were to be transferred thither.[4]
Charlemagne likewise felt himself to be commissioned by
Christ: when he took his place on the imperial throne in
the cathedral at Aachen, the mosaic of the enthroned Christ
in the dome was concealed by a vault.[5] The political divine
grace of the Western ruler hovered very close to the divine
kingship Constantine had made Christian: the enthroned
Christ who sanctioned Christian sovereignty was in practice
always in danger—as in the mosaic at Aachen—of being
thrust out of sight by his earthly representative.

In the words of one of the later Byzantine patriarchs,
shortly before 1400, the Roman Emperor still formed an in-
separable unity and community with the Church, being
endowed with something like a super-hierarchical authority,
not only over the Church of Constantinople, but also over
the so-called autocephalous patriarchs.[6] It was in virtue of
this authority that he called popes to judgment before him

up to the seventh century; Gregory the Great even invoked this right against himself in order not to have to mount the papal throne.

In theory, of course, the Emperor was regarded solely as "bishop for external affairs" of the Church (ἐπίσκοπος τῶν ἐκτός); but these external affairs included at times—especially on serious and momentous occasions—such important matters as the creation of dioceses, the appointment of ecclesiastical dignitaries and often even questions of doctrine. From the standpoint of this imperial practice, the subjection of the Sicilian and Illyrian Church under the patriarchs of Constantinople in the eighth century was an absolutely lawful act of the Emperor's ecclesiastical sovereignty; the assertion of independence on the part of the Roman papacy an unlawful infringement of it.

The ecumenical councils, above all, were developed by the Emperor so that they became a court of final appeal within the scheme of Church-government: he called them together, presided over them and published their conclusions—that is, he endowed these with the force of law. Behind the formal autonomy of the Church, it was the Emperor who was active and who made the decision whenever this was required. The proof that even Rome for a long time could not imagine any other form of Church-government may be seen in the fact that so single-minded a pope as Leo the Great, after preparing with the utmost energy for the Council of Chalcedon (451), finally left it to the Emperor to call it together.

The change of emphasis in Church-consciousness is reflected also in the gradual development of the interior of the church-building, as we can see very clearly from some of the models in the Byzantine museum in Athens. Out of the ancient Christian basilica, which was completely public, there emerged as a midway stage the *Hagia Sophia* and then, later, the domed, cruciform church. Gradually the liturgy was deprived of this public character, taking place at first beyond the choir-stalls and finally—particularly in Russia—behind a closed iconostasis. What remained as a public part of the church—the lay-church—lost its character as a *way* and became a static circular-shaped or polygon-shaped place in the midst of which the imperial symbol of the eagle represented the "vicar of Christ". Christ became visible preeminently in the medium of sovereignty; hence he appeared also in the dome-mosaics of the apses as the enthroned Christ-King.

5. What was mainly interesting about this enthroned Christ, seen first of all in contrast to *dominus Caesar* as divine lord, was still his divinity. For his function was to make dominion as far as possible divine. Even if the Egyptian and late Roman deifying of the ruler could not be maintained, nevertheless Christ as God granting and indeed delegating sovereignty assured a gift of divine grace which could be linked directly with ancient oriental traditions and make dominion itself and all that came into contact with it "holy" or "sacred" : sacred majesty, the holy empire, even the sacred bedchamber. For this reason, after Arius had questioned the divinity of Christ in Constantine's time, the emperors gave up supporting his heresy—with the aid of which they might have hoped for a time to maintain the primacy of the "divine Caesar" over the mere man, Christ—and became then the inflexible champions of Christ's divinity.

From the standpoint of dogma, they were in fact upholding a weak form of Monophysitism; an opinion which the emperors were inclined to favour, because Monophysite tendencies among their subjects in Syria and Egypt were threatening to split the imperial Church. In spite of the correct emphasis given at the Council of Chalcedon in 451 to the notion of the union of the divine and *human* natures in Christ, it is his divinity which since then has remained uppermost in Christian consciousness. Jesus Christ became simply Christ, a kind of double of the Father : a situation which made it possible for Luther in his day to play with the idea of an almost metaphysical duplication of God, conceiving the Old Testament as the revelation of the Father's anger and the New of the Son's love.

The same process was repeated in the Middle Ages, when Berengarius of Tours questioned the real presence of Christ in the Blessed Sacrament and the Albigensians described this as "mere bread". The reaction on the part of the defenders of the real—particularly the divine—presence was so strong that it gave rise to what was known as Christological nihilism, according to which Christ was considered solely as God, his humanity composed of body and soul as separate and not properly definable (*non aliquid = nihil*).[7] This doctrine was condemned by Alexander III, but how closely it corresponded to the contemporary outlook is evident from the fact that in the later Middle Ages the Eucharist was quite widely called simply "God".[8]

Even when, in the later Middle Ages, the almost forgotten other half of the truth of the Incarnation came again into sight, it was no longer possible to bring it into the right relationship with the first, that is, to make men aware of the central position of the divine-human union. The Franciscan movement succeeded only in making Jesus in his poverty and suffering as such an object for compassion or imitation; in practice, this aided the slow decline of Christianity to the secularized plane of humanitarianism. Moreover, Mary grew in stature beyond all the other saints, becoming a new central figure—a process, however, which was interrupted by the sharp reaction of the Reformation.

6. A momentous accentuation of the position of the clergy in the hierarchical structure of the Church was brought about by the fact that Constantine made their various grades correspond to the grades of the State hierarchy. Thus the patriarchs came to correspond to the four *praefecti*, the metropolitans to provincial governors, while the bishops

began to also to take up important secular positions as a result of the decline of local administration. In addition, the clergy received considerable State privileges, such as freedom from public burdens and even certain judicial offices—notably that of arbitrator. As a result of this parallelism and privileged status, by way of substitution for the declining or ineffective power of the State, a political dominion of bishops and popes was able to emerge. Their rise to power in difficult times, during imperial crises and invasions, was naturally welcomed by their subjects: we can trace it, for instance, in certain traits in the legend of the popular saint, Nicholas of Myra; in the measures taken by Gregory I to defend Rome, cut off from the metropolitan city of Constantinople and threatened by the barbarians; finally, in the taking over of municipal government by the Frankish bishops in Merovingian times. But what concerns us here is not so much the political development as the ecclesiastical aspect of the process. As a result of the Constantinian turning-point, the clergy, hitherto unquestionably first and foremost the representatives of the Christian people in face of the persecuting State, were torn away from this anchorage and established in principle above them, holding an authority similar to and in association with that of the State hierarchy: a situation which inevitably diminished their sacred character. The momentous consequence has been that, since then, a natural unity between clergy and people emerged only in times of danger or persecution; in normal times the laity felt that their emotional needs were better appreciated by members of the religious orders.

Although historically inevitable, the Constantinian turning-point therefore cannot be regarded as an unmixed blessing for the Church. It was not long before a movement to resist its dangerous possibilities made itself felt, both expressly in the sphere of ecclesiastical politics—as, for example, by

Athanasius—and in the field of theology and philosophy—as by Augustine. Nevertheless, after the experience of the per-secutions—which is generally presented in too idealistic a light—it can be understood that the Constantinian turning-point was on the whole greeted with joy. The ending of the illegal status of the Church, the guarantee on the part of Christian rulers to maintain Christianity by force as the uni-versal religion, finally the position of authority and economic security held by the hierarchy: these things provided suffi-cient reason not to make an occasional dispute with the State into one of principle.

Only in the West, where Roman rule soon gave way to a variety of short-lived Germanic local sovereignties, did the position of the Church become so important that it was able to gain both greater freedom at every stage and in principle a greater self-confidence. Here the Church slowly grew out of the Constantinian amalgam with the Empire to rise as a power above both imperial and local rulers, as Isidore of Seville already noted.[9] The clergy began to set up a parallel between themselves and the prophets of Israel and to inter-vene in political questions.[10] But even in the West it was a long time before these trends ripened into a complete plan to change the basic structure, being held in check through the period of the Carolingians and the Ottos. The full conse-quences were drawn only by the reforming popes of the eleventh century.

Anticipating a little here, we have to point out that this decision of the Roman papacy was realized in the form of a break with the Byzantine imperial Church. Nevertheless, the official claim of the Orthodox Church—which represents also the view of many Western Christians—to have upheld on this occasion the authentic and ancient tradition of the Church must be rejected. No matter how far back into the first Christian centuries its traditions of faith and worship may reach, its situation as a whole was radically changed—

as we have seen—by the Constantinian turning-point and the resultant formation of an imperial State Church. On the other hand, Rome could rightly appeal to a more ancient status, to a tradition which it had better preserved and to the beginnings of a properly ecclesiastical sovereignty. Admittedly, even the reform which it brought into existence—like every Reformation—did not in the end re-establish an older historical situation but created a new one.

When Charlemagne laid the permanent foundations of a new Europe, he took over the structure of a Christianity, with its political and philosophical heritage, which had been firmly established through the decisions of later Roman times. Western Christianity was therefore an ecclesiastical and cultural unity. Charlemagne, aided by a novel political interpretation of Augustinian ideas, felt himself to be lord of the *Civitas Dei* in this world and therefore responsible alike for the state of the Empire and for the state of the Christian Church and Christian culture. For all these tasks the clergy were also at his disposal, among them the Benedictine monks who had long represented the Christian cultural amalgam of Europe. It is in the adoption of the ecclesiastical and cultural traditions, no matter how modest the extent of these may be, that Charlemagne's historical significance lies. It included the creative achievement of mobilizing the Frankish peoples for this undertaking and putting a new field at their disposal in the form of a Europe in the process of development. In this transplanting or—to use the medieval term—*translatio*, it was of course inevitable that the contents of the late Roman tradition would be considerably transformed by the outlook of those who took them over. There will be more to say about this in later chapters.

Before that, we must examine the historical consequences of the new situation created by Charlemagne. By transplanting the late Roman traditions to new peoples and regions—

that is, by a *translatio* which went far beyond the *translatio imperii* understood in a purely political sense—Charlemagne abandoned the ecumenicity of the Roman Empire still existing at Constantinople. He created—so to speak—a double of this, finding it opportune to base himself on the old imperial capital of Rome and—by being crowned as Emperor in the year 800—to be able to rouse again the memory of the once flourishing Western half of the Roman Empire.

None of the earlier Germanic princes had been able to set themselves up in this way alongside the Roman Empire of the East; hence, even in Constantinople it had been possible to maintain the fiction of an *oecumene* ruled by the Emperor there, in spite of the actual loss of the West. There, people had always distinguished between the one Emperor and the many kings and considered the latter as belonging to the imperial family and thus in a loose way dependent on him. But now a genuine rival had arisen in the Carolingian domain and, by taking on the imperial form, had laid an explicit claim to ecumenicity. It is not our task here to elucidate the hasty agreement in the peace of 813 by the two emperors on their claims to ecumenicity; it was, in any case, soon to be outdated by events. But we must point to the fact—far more important historically—that Charlemagne did not assert his claim for the first time at the coronation in Rome in 800, but already some years earlier—and indeed in the ecclesiastical sphere—at his Council at Frankfurt in 794. The situation was favourable on both occasions. In Constantinople a woman was reigning and Charlemagne tried, as the true successor of Constantine, to fill the vacant office of *vicarius Dei*.

Charlemagne was not particularly interested in the object of this Council of Frankfurt—which was to decide against the conclusions reached at the earlier seventh ecumenical Council held in the East in 787—although it may be observed that, like the Byzantine emperors at the time of the

Iconoclast controversy, he took up a position *opposed* to the cult of images of the saints. But it was more important to him to raise an objection to a definition of an ecumenical council and to attempt to revise this definition—hitherto considered irrevocable—by means of an ecumenical council of his own. If he had succeeded in this effort, the established Roman imperial Church would have been replaced by a new Frankish imperial Church. But since Constantinople naturally did not recognize the Council of Frankfurt, Charlemagne was only able to gain a lesser object, namely, to destroy the existing constitution of the Church.[11] The West had dispensed with the old Roman Emperor, but he had also dispensed with the West. Even before the acknowledged schism in the Church and before the proclamation of the Emperor in 800, the separation of the Western from the Eastern Church was therefore decided. The hitherto existing form of ecumenical dominion over the Church on the part of the Emperor had ceased to function : there were now two *oecumenes*, that is, in reality none at all.

The fact that an ecumenical Church constitution no longer existed was recognized by the Orthodox Church in as much as it no longer counted its synods after 787 as general councils. Similarly, the Emperors of the West called their general Church assemblies synods, even when they reached such important decisions as, for instance, those of Sutri in 1046. The popes of Rome did indeed try through their measures of reform to re-establish the ecumenicity of the Church's constitution under their spiritual leadership : hence, even from the time of the Lateran synods in Rome in the twelfth century, they described the ecclesiastical assemblies which they had themselves convened as councils.

Actually the popes now remained the sole claimants to universal headship over the Western Church, after the imperial dignity under the Ottos had become a German affair and the decisions of emperors in ecclesiastical affairs met with increasing opposition from the non-German countries of the West. But the popes never again succeeded in establishing their claim outside Western Europe. The ecclesiastical schism between East and West was smouldering even from the time of the coronation of Otto the Great as Emperor in 962[12] and could no longer be averted when a straightforward claim by the Pope to the primacy took the place of the actually existent dual imperial sovereignty; for this did not mean merely a *de facto* attack on the Byzantine imperial Church, as it might have been on a Frankish or German Church, but an attack on the very principle behind it.

Repeated negotiations in difficult times between the Eastern emperors and the Pope for the union of the Churches could not succeed in face of the opposition—which has persisted to the present time—of the faithful in the East, accustomed to the imperial Church, and later of the Russian State. Thus the ecumenicity of the papal government, claiming a dogmatic basis and recognized in the Middle Ages by all the West, never established itself historically outside the sphere of the Roman Church; in this respect it was as unsuccessful as the so-called reform councils set up in accordance with the conciliar theory in the fifteenth century.

V

The Heirs: The Germanic Miracle-world

THE Germanic peoples—in fact, mainly Franks, Anglo-Saxons and Normans—became the creators of a new histori-cal unity in Europe. In an analysis of the content of "Euro-pean cultural values" we must look first of all to the legacy of Antiquity and Christianity; but we cannot ignore the achievement of the heirs without running the risk of turning past history into ideology. It is true that, in our present state of historical and cultural upheaval, we might be for-given for not raising this other decisive question of the agent in the historical process—of the heir to the tradition. But a catalogue of traditions and values, even if these are described as "supra-temporal", offers no assurance that those who shape the course of history will stake their existence on them and so endow them with historical validity and perman-ence. If the Germans had not accepted Christianity and had not been receptive to the learning of the ancient world, what we know as Western Christianity or Western Civilization would simply not have existed. The "supra-temporal values" of Antiquity and Christianity might then perhaps have com-pleted faded out; at any rate they would not have lived on in Europe. But this also means that Europe itself would have been completely different.

This decisive participation of the Germanic peoples—of paramount historical importance in Ranke's triad, even sur-passing that of Antiquity or Christianity—had to be noted from the beginning, particularly as it enters into our theme only to a modest extent and—as such—in a more or less negative fashion. If the historical perspective is not to be distorted, there must be a thorough and positive evaluation of their real contribution before the further observation be made that the Germans brought no sort of fund of ideas comparable to Antiquity and Christianity when they entered with these into a common destiny.

It is here precisely that the importance of this aspect of the course of history lies: the Germanic peoples reached the heights of their own cultural achievement only as the heirs of Antiquity and Christianity. Their capacity even to do this must not be under-estimated; otherwise, however, all that they brought as their own contribution was a peasant-culture—worthy of respect indeed, but scarcely of equal value—and a lofty tribal and warrior-ethos. Both must be regarded as "archaic" and cannot be given an unduly high rank among cultural values—as the advocates of racial policy tried to do when they wanted to shut out Antiquity and Christianity. We must repeat: the importance of the Germanic peoples in world-history lies in the fact that they were ready to accept the historical heritage of Christianity and the ancient world and in this contact demonstrated their own power to create a new civilization.

The question of European Christianity is here reduced, then, to that of the way in which the Germanic peoples became Christian. In the late Roman Empire Christianity had adopted and sometimes developed transmissible cultural forms, such as public worship, the conceptual structure of patristic theology and the shape and contours of the Constantinian Empire. These forms were indeed taken over also into the Germanic world, but their maintenance was in the hands of particular groups—notably of the monks and the palace nobility—whom Charlemagne expressly appointed for the task. But the great mass of the population was only passively engaged, listening and obeying.

Their readiness for this passive acceptance indicates that

45

Christianity had already touched them more closely : some aspects of Christianity must have been able to be taken over without effort—so to speak—into the familiar world of their primitive imagination. We know, for instance, that the first Christian epics written in Old High German—particularly the *Heliand*, but also Otfrid's *Krist*—represent such a *translatio* of Christianity into the imaginative world of the Germanic warriors. It need scarcely be added that this involves also a transformation of the Christian tradition : things which had been considered of central importance to Christianity, as for example humility or the silent endurance of injustice, are now removed to the periphery or simply not taken over at all; others, such as feudal loyalty or active resistance to evil, come to the fore—even emerge for the first time out of a primitive world to enter into a new existence in a Christian context.

We are not, however, concerned with the details of literary analysis : what we have to do is to keep in mind the central fact which decisively impressed the Germanic tribes when they accepted Christianity. About this there is no possible doubt : the God of the Christians had shown himself to be the stronger God. This argument held naturally for the political leaders in the first place, those who, like Constantine, had conquered in his name; for we must not forget that Christianity was adopted mainly by the ruling class. But the simple people also could not fail to be convinced by the power of a God in whose name the Donar Oak was felled, without the indwelling God doing anything to prevent it, and who alone protected the Christian missionaries coming as strangers and solitaries through the dangerous and lonely forests. From this experience of the stronger God it was easy to find a way to the picture of Christ enthroned in glory, which the Byzantine imperial Church bequeathed to the Germanic peoples.

Ordinary life for the Germanic peoples went on within the tribal confines more or less without concern for the gods. These lived indeed in a world which formed a distant background to the present, but normal life and above all morals were scarcely touched by it. On the other hand, what kept the Germans under direct and constant pressure was the extraordinary sense of fate, conceived almost as a personal being,[1] the gods might then be regarded as allies against this Fate, and naturally each tribe appealed to them in worship and sought their favourable judgment in battle. But an individual or a group might also enter by agreement into a closer association with a God. It was in this way, for example, at the time of the great migrations, that Wotan, the god of the warrior-bands, gained precedence over the old sky-god, Ziu. On the basis of such an agreement, made in a simple form, the God in question was drawn into the earthly existence of the individual or group and was expected to further the interests of his contractual partner: in other words, to provide aid and success. If the God did not act as such a "friend in need", his client was very ready to change his allegiance or to abandon it altogether.[2]

They turned in the same way from the heathen gods to the stronger Christ. Naturally he commended himself to them, not so much in his suffering and love as in his power as heavenly king bringing salvation. Although the political leaders and their immediate entourage were the first to be converted in this way to Christianity, this fact alone worked as a powerful stimulus on their subjects who were only too glad to be brought with them also more directly under the Christian God. When the Carolingians had accomplished their reform of the Church, they felt themselves to be fully responsible for the Christian status of their subjects, with the result that the last remnants of paganism were extinguished—if necessary, as in the wars against the Saxons, by the use of massive political power.

47

The Germanic peoples were thus faced with a new situation in their relationship to God. In the first place, the association with the Christian God was binding on everyone without exception; and, in the second, it could no longer be exchanged in favour of another God. When this relationship was made universal and stable, instead of being—as previously—a merely possible and temporary obligation, it could be borne by the Germans only if its fruits also became universal and permanent. In other words, the Christian God had to reveal himself less as the announcer of salvation to come than as the guarantor of every earthly success. He had to show that he was above the course of earthly destiny by an uninterrupted series of interventions from the world beyond, in brief, to present himself as the great miracle-worker. The atmosphere of primitive Germanic Christianity could therefore only be that of belief in the miraculous, the hourly expectation of supernatural events. The generalization of this kind of faith is the distinguishing mark of Western Christianity in its early stages by comparison with both the older Church and the Germanic past. The historical sources of this period report more miracles than events which we would today consider to be history in the proper sense. People were even more ready to believe reports of miracles than to trust their own sight: if they did not in fact see a miracle supposed to have been worked in their presence, they assumed that for some reason they had not been worthy to do so.

Naturally, this universal expectation of miracles looked for more immediate and personal assurances than merely that of Christ alone enthroned in distant majesty. If the Christian faith was to be accepted and firmly established, it simply had to provide in the band of saints innumerable mediators who as human beings were close to those looking for aid and, being now in heavenly glory, were also close to him who granted it. At this point the ancient Christian cult of the saints, emerging victorious after the Iconoclast controversy and approved by the Church, found a fruitful soil in the world of the newly converted Germanic peoples. But there was a change of emphasis. The early Church venerated the saints mainly as fellow wayfarers who had gone in advance and now reached their goal in heaven; in the primitive northern world, they were predominantly superior miracle-workers who in given circumstances demonstrated the power of Christ their Master. But that these miracles had a solid, earthly meaning and that the saints were invoked mainly as helpers in time of need is quite clear from medieval accounts and legends of the saints.

By way of illustration two examples may be cited: today they may seem to be extreme, but in fact they belong to a quite high intellectual level. The first is from the Frankish historian, Gregory of Tours, and is particularly instructive as an indication that this prince of the Church and scion of a noble Roman family was already under the influence of the belief in miracles dominant in his Germanic environment. He praises the powder rubbed away from a saint's tombstone in these words: "O divine purgative, superior to all doctor's recipes, which cleanses the belly like scammony and washes away all stains from our conscience."[3] There is already a touch of intellectual superiority in the other example, taken from the account in the *Legenda Aurea* of miracles worked after death by St Martin of Tours. A blind man and a cripple, who had become rich by begging, fearing lest a chance miracle deprive them of their income, hastily left their house on the day when the saint's body was being carried in solemn procession to his church in that neighbourhood. But they were too late, came right into the way of the procession, "and because God giveth many benefits to men not desired, and that would not have them, they were both healed against their will, and were right sorry therefor".[4]

It might be observed that this faith in miracles was characteristic of the ordinary people, while theology—even in

49

Carolingian times—Notker's Sequences, and quite certainly Scholasticism were on a very different plane. That is precisely our own opinion; but we are concerned with the Christianity of the ordinary people. And it has to be recognized that, broadly speaking, they determine the sociological pattern of the Middle Ages. Theology and hymns were the concern of smaller groups which had far less direct influence on their contemporaries than it might seem when we study solely the documents of a superior tradition. There is a danger in all studies of the literature of a period—and therefore also in the historical method—of exaggerating its influence on real life. The broad basis of European Christianity is represented by this faith in miracles and not by theology: interest in theology on the part of the masses was only aroused for the first time by the controversies of the Reformation period. The spiritual and intellectual level even of the average cleric remained very limited and scarcely permitted him to do more than convey the rudiments of the Christian faith; hence it may be asked: "what spiritual influence could these have exercised on the faithful, whose barbarism, ignorance and brutality even exceeded their own?"[5]

If we assert that faith in miracles is the predominant characteristic of German Christianity, this must be understood as no more than the observation of a historical fact and not as the product of an analysis of the essential nature of the Germanic soul. We are not maintaining that this kind of faith could only arise there: that would be to revive the racial ideology in a negative form and would mean isolating the facts above-mentioned. It was not only among the Germanic peoples that faith in miracles was common and it was not rooted in any particular racial quality. The same reservation will have to be made when, at a later stage, we speak of the moral contribution of the Celts. The new attitude of mind may perhaps be seen in the way in which at an early date relics were transported—those of St Andrew, for instance, to Constantinople (357) or as Ambrose had them brought to Milan; and it is certain that the world in which Pope Gregory the Great lived was already characterized largely by faith in miracles and an emphasis on moral effort.

In this connection we might speak of a rebarbarizing of the ancient civilization from the third century onwards. But this is probably not to be assessed simply for its own sake, but in connection with the fact that Christianity had become universal by the time of Constantine or at any rate of Theodosius. The masses were not able to bear the continual tension of Christianity, firmly held by the transitory earthly life on the one hand and on the other orientated to the mysterious end of all things: the tendency to find relief through faith in miracles and moral exertion was therefore particularly strong.

Regarded historically, the "people" lives in a primitive world (whether this judgment needs modification for our technical age cannot be discussed here). The less the Roman Empire and Roman law succeeded in submitting mankind in the early Middle Ages to a rational discipline, the more did the primitive natural tendencies proliferate on the surface of history. On the other hand, the more the imperial idea of the Carolingians and the Ottos gained ground among the nobility, the bishops and their vassals, so much the more were these trends held back even in the Germanic and the later German world. To this extent the late medieval faith in miracles may be regarded as the price which had to be paid for the uncompromising struggle of the reform-Church against the Emperor and nobility: we need not be surprised that a new wave of faith in miracles set in from the late tenth century precisely in the Burgundian-Aquitanian world which Cluny made the first base for the working out of its ideas of religious reform.[6] But the effect of the reform initiated by the monastery of Cluny was two-sided. On the one hand, it recognized the fact of the return to a barbaric and primitive state and provided suitable outlets in miracles and in pilgrimages. On the other hand, it tried to impose discipline, especially on the nobility, but also on the ordinary people, and thus prepared the West for an inward assimilation of Christianity.

It is, however, significant and decisive that this end was to be attained by a subjective deepening of the faith in miracles. By the special intensity of its worship and by a display of splendour Cluny brought the traditional liturgy again to the notice of the local nobility, but thus also to that of wider circles. This was brought about, not only by the extension and enrichment of the liturgical services, but also by two liturgical innovations: the daily singing of the litany of the saints before the High Mass and the introduction of the daily solemn Requiem Mass. The linking of the litany of the saints with the central liturgy of the Mass brought back into unity the world of heavenly miracle-workers, which had been split up into innumerable local cults, and restored their ministerial status. Over this unity there presided the Queen of heaven, whose ascendancy over all other saints began at this time, so that she was soon able to act to some extent as representative of the rest.

More important, however, was the linking of the new feast of All Souls with the already established feast of All Saints, a product of the Iconoclast struggle. This feast and its prolongation in the daily liturgy of the dead mark the point at which medieval man, entangled in earthly pursuits, was not only emotionally and casually awakened to the traditional world of official worship, but also existentially and permanently involved. The massive world of earthly interests, demanding over and above the application of one's own life also the assurance of aid from innumerable saints, was so to speak surpassed and inwardly emptied by a central interest putting all others in the shade: the salvation of one's soul. And not only one's own soul, but also the souls of relatives and dependants—as was obvious in a world of clan-membership, particularly in that of the nobility. Cluny followed up this interest inasmuch as the monks interceded for their living relatives in the world through the brotherhood of prayer and for the deceased through the regular office of the dead.

The Reformation did an historical injustice in denouncing this service of the dead as a "coarsening" of Christianity. From the historical point of view, it was much rather a sublimation of still coarser origins; it was also to be ascribed more to the Germanic outlook than to the Roman Church as such. But it must be admitted that this interest in the salvation of the soul did not completely supersede the world of earthly interests. The system of "private churches" (*Eigen-kirchentum*) was not contested in principle by Cluny, but only the possession of such churches by lay-people. Anything "worldly" appeared to be justified without further argument as long as there was some ecclesiastical connection: in this way the reform brought about an ecclesiastical positivism which, in the liturgy, took on a ritual form. For this also was undertaken under the old Roman perspective of *do ut des*.[7]

What made the greatest impression in this reform and took the central place was the office of the dead, which predominated over the other services. It is of course a great historical achievement that on Sundays and Holy Days the ancient Christian liturgy was handed down for more than a thousand years; but we must not overlook the fact that it was passed on in a language unintelligible to the people and that when the sermon was later introduced this did not so much interpret the spirit of the liturgy as emphasize the importance of salvation and arouse moral efforts. It was the liturgical movement at the beginning of the twentieth century which first revived the early Christian consciousness as embodied in the liturgy—and even then only to a modest degree. Previously, this larger Christian reality had been practically buried under the dread of death and judgment, which had found striking expression in the *Dies Irae* and in this form had entered into the much more restrained ancient liturgy of the dead.

Against this background, the effect of the new discovery of Mary's ascendancy as Queen of heaven was to make her more the intercessor at the judgment than the first-born of creation elevated by grace; and the reality of the sacraments was to a large extent concentrated in practice on forgiveness of sins and gaining indulgences. At a much later date Nietzsche could still make the illuminating comment on the Protestants of his own time, who had long abandoned medieval practices: "They ought to look more redeemed, these redeemed ones."

The subjective deepening of faith in miracles ran parallel with an objective deepening which appeared somewhat later. In order to understand it, we have to return again to the multi-coloured world of the heavenly friends in need and—more especially—ask about the materialization which this had found in the world of earthly events. For the sake of comparison, we may recall that this materialization took on the form of the icon in the Byzantine world and it is significant that there too the materialization of iconostasis more and more concealed the central liturgical event, the latter finally being withdrawn almost completely from the sight of the congregation. At the same time this abundance of icons was always linked with the central icon of Christ himself and derived its validity from the belief that these pictures of Christ were genuine likenesses ("true photographs", as we might say to make the point clear), all of which could be traced back to two pictures supposed to belong to Christ's own time and still available at the beginning of iconography.[8] It is therefore understandable that the type of the picture of Christ could not be altered or left to the artist's discretion. From this obligatory canon in regard to the picture of Christ there emerged a rigid scheme for the icons of saints, with the result that iconography retained for centuries a static character: the real liberation of art came about when this rigidity began to be broken down in the West from the thirteenth century.

In virtue of the ancient Greek idea that the subject was present in his likeness, the icons were regarded as a part of the heavenly world projected into the earthly. They were venerated as an essential element of the divine liturgy. We in the Roman Church can appreciate their meaning for orthodoxy only in the light of the idea of "sacramental presence", which for us is centred in the Eucharist. Only in this way can we understand the passions aroused by the Iconoclast controversy in the Byzantine Church; only in this way also see why iconostasis could in the end conceal the liturgical action at the altar from the view of the congregation. For these found the "sacramental presence" already in the icons before the priest realized it in the liturgy. In the Roman Church likewise at a later date the liturgy was "concealed from the people" by the use of Latin;[9] nevertheless, it was always maintained that there was no sacramental presence other than that mediated by the priest. Hence, even when the clergy were screened off from the rest, the Church upheld the full visibility of the liturgical act in the congregational service and from the thirteenth century emphasized the central point of the liturgy through the elevation of the Host after the consecration. But then the Eucharist also as a permanent sacrament became like the icons the object of a special veneration to which the liturgy was secondary.[10]

That is not to say that Eucharistic piety can be derived historically from the veneration of icons. What we can describe in theological terms as the distinctive doctrines of the Greek and Roman Churches is the result of an historical break which took place first of all on another level. In place of images—which Charlemagne already at his Council of Frankfurt wanted to restrict to a commemorative and ornamental role—we have in the Western Church relics: it is

E   55

from these and not from icons that the direct historical line leads to the Eucharist. It is evident from the fact that the procession with the Host grew out of the procession with relics (in as much as the Host was borne as an adjunct to these)[11] and that the same Lateran Council which formulated in 1215 the doctrine of Transubstantiation in another chapter (62) condemned abuses in the veneration of relics.

In the more material Germanic world relics meant precisely what in the more spiritual Byzantine world icons were intended to be: that part of heaven which was already present and perceptible on earth. As we are now accustomed to distinguish between the dead body of the saint and that which will be glorified after the resurrection, we are no longer able to understand how the faith of that age identified these as a matter of course. For the Middle Ages it was a question of *the same* body in which the saint, now in heaven, declared his presence among his admirers. This he did in the form of ever new miracles, even—as we saw from the legend of St Martin—in miracles worked against the wishes of the beneficiaries. Also everything which had come into contact with the body of the saint—his clothes, objects used by him and even his gravestone—shared in this miraculous power.

There was no end to the number of the saints, still less to that of their miracles. But in practice this miracle-world was simplified by the fact that the cult was concentrated on local saints in whom the proximity of the heavenly world was assured in a completely concrete fashion for those who lived in a particular area. Saints of more than local importance scarcely roused any great interest in the first Germanic centuries. Naturally an exception must be made for some of the apostles, such as John, devotion to whom was spread by the Irish monks, or Peter, who soon acquired universal respect— but most of all in France—as the key-bearer of heaven.[12] But among the native saints the great miracle-worker Martin of Tours was almost the only one who gained more than local veneration, though we must perhaps recall that his cloak (*capella*) was kept in the "chapel" of the Frankish kings and solemnly venerated as a State possession. It was only with a more thorough christianization, the concentration of settlements and the participation in the wider problems of the Church that a canon of the great saints came to be established, these being then recognized as above all the others and adopted—for example—as patrons of churches. But for a long time yet the grave of the local saint remained in the foreground of the cult. When there was no such local saint available or at least could not be found in the neighbourhood, every means—even to the extent of stealing relics—was adopted to provide one. At the time of Lewis the Pious (778-840), for instance, there was a wave of relic-transference which drew on the fantasy and will-power of the young Western world at least as fully as—for example—the consolidation of landed property. Soon the bodies of the saints began to be placed in golden display shrines, the making of which remained one of the main tasks of Western art up to Gothic times. Recalling the Old Testament, they were known as the ark of the covenant.[13] Out of this context, there emerged finally the practice of making pilgrimages to the graves and shrines of saints: the greatest of these, putting all others completely in the shade, being to Santiago de Compostela at the outermost edge of the Christian World.

It must be pointed out that this form of venerating the saints was more than a matter of interest to the individual or the Church and had also an important political meaning. This can be seen for the first time in the transference of the relics of St Andrew to Constantinople, already in 357 charged with political significance, which then in the ninth century under Photius led to the legendary exaltation of Andrew over Peter —ὁ πρὸ Πέτρου Πέτρος—and thus to the justification of claims to primacy in the Church.[14] The possession of the body of a saint was a pledge of heavenly aid also for the medieval

57

states—above all, for those which were young and weak and therefore most in need of help. Thus the resistance of the small Spanish remainder-state against the Moors in the ninth century was concentrated on Santiago, while at the same time the still youthful state of Venice looked to San Marco; in the tenth century the new Christian states in Bohemia and Poland found their spiritual centres in St Wenceslaus and St Adalbert. But even the greater states had to restore with the aid of saints the prestige of sacredness which had been shaken by the Investiture controversy.

France, which had been least concerned in this dispute, had the good fortune to possess St Denis from of old and Abbot Suger gave him a new importance. England in the same twelfth century gained in St Edward and St Thomas à Becket new heavenly patrons, while Germany—admittedly in a more dubious fashion—adopted Charlemagne. Moreover, from the very beginning of the Christian State, crowns and other insignia—which of course could not hold a whole saint—were adorned with smaller relics and thus given supernatural powers. The Emperor Constantine had the nails from Christ's cross placed in his helmet and bridle. It is also said that the crown found in the grave of Charlemagne contained a piece of the wood of the cross and probably his throne at Aachen also held a relic. The head of the lance of St Maurice, belonging to the time of the Saxon rulers, was likewise fitted with a nail from the cross of Christ: this and a piece of the wood of the cross were later inserted into the imperial cross of Conrad II which today can be seen in Vienna.[15]

It is no exaggeration to say that the devotion of the ordinary people in the Middle Ages was roused mainly by the cult of relics. On the other hand, the liturgical and properly sacramental acts were matters of obligation: participation in these had first to be commanded. But images also, which for the Eastern Church provided the location of a sacramental presence, in the West never had any function other than instructive and ornamental: here relics occupied the place of the sacramental presence. Charlemagne had it expressly noted in the *Libri Carolini* that images could be assimilated neither to the Scriptures nor to relics in their claim to veneration.[16] Soon there were not enough bodies of saints to supply the increasing numbers of churches and altars and "particles" had to suffice. The importance of relics was still evident at the time when Calvinism began, opening its attack very often with a "storming of images". This did not mean solely or even primarily the destruction of pictorial representations— as we might think in our aesthetic age—but above all the profanation and dispersion of relics. It had been preceded by the less noisy and less pathetic "removal of the abuse of relics" in the Lutheran and Anglican Churches. On the other hand in the Roman Church after the Counter-Reformation, in the baroque age, the cult of relics experienced a grandiose second bloom.

It would be easy to prove that there were relics also in the Eastern Church, in earlier times even considerably more than in the West; on the other hand, that there were also images in the Roman Church and, in the later Middle Ages, even considerably more than in the Byzantine world. But our observations are not concerned with mere statistics. In order to understand decisive historical processes, it is not important so much to know what was *also* involved, but what was primarily involved and thus served as the locus of crystallization for many other things and for the conduct of life. If we stick to enumerations of equal importance, we reach general conclusions which may be useful for anthropology but historically speaking are "empty".

From the standpoint of anthropology, the fact that there were relics in Byzantium and images in the West is a subdivision of the much more universal phenomena of reverence for the dead and of image-ornaments. But the important thing from the historical point of view is the form in which at a particular time such more universal phenomena appeared, still more where and when they came to the foreground of historical existence, so as to give to this its special character and to draw other phenomena under its influence. From this point of view, we must admit that in Byzantium icons and in the West relics held the central place in religious life and feeling. In both instances it was a question of phenomena escaping out of the given background of the liturgical action, where everything was drawn into the act of worship, and leading to an objectifying and materializing cult which set those who offered it at a distance from the sacred object and at least momentarily absorbed their self-consciousness. It is here alone that the historical line can be perceived leading from the cult of relics to the prominence of the Eucharist in the Middle Ages.

If we compare the early Christian and the medieval conceptions of the Eucharist merely on the theological level, there is a complete antithesis which Henri de Lubac has examined at length in his book on the *Corpus Mysticum*.[17] In the early Church the sacrament of the body and blood of our Lord was called "the mystical body", but from the late Middle Ages it has been known as "the true body" (*corpus reale*); on the other hand, the term "mystical body" was transferred to what had formerly been called simply "the body of Christ" (*corpus Christi*) and became the name of the Church which celebrates the liturgy.

This complete transformation of the traditional terminology must have passed over intermediate stages and it is the great merit of de Lubac to have indicated these in the theological field. But in my opinion it would be a mistake to discover the intermediate stages leading to the new terminology merely in the evolution of theological concepts or even to suppose that this theological development was the main reason for the emergence in both public worship and private devotion in the Middle Ages of a picture so different from that of the early Church. Some of de Lubac's remarks seem to indicate a theory of this kind, which in my opinion tends to place the historical events in a false light.

We must in fact learn to appreciate—and we have already pointed this out several times—the fact that theology as such is the principle behind historical processes to a far lesser degree than its importance for the development of doctrine might lead us to suppose. Much more often theology develops side by side with historical events and quite independently of these or it follows on them as the expression of something else which is itself more likely to become the principle of historical action. This is a living faith which emerges—so to speak—out of a scarcely perceptible background and compels also the formation of theological ideas. The decisive factor in the understanding of medieval Christianity is that not only theology, but also faith itself became transformed, although both dogma and cult remained essentially the same.[18]

A transformation of this kind cannot be explained mainly in terms of a theological development. Theology anyway remained on the whole remote from the interests of the Germans right up to the time of the Reformation, although from the Carolingian renaissance onwards there were relatively small minorities which showed an astonishing grasp of the teaching of the Fathers. Much more fundamental, therefore, to the historical appreciation of the Middle Ages is the living Christianity of the ordinary people. But already in late antiquity after the compulsory conversion of imperial subjects and still more after the return to barbarism as a result of the Germanic and Slav settlements, this Christianity had become de-liturgized and materialized. The process, which affected the Eastern Church in the form of the cult of icons, was turned in the West into a cult of relics. For this objectified piety it was decisive that in the icon as in the relic the saint who was venerated was "really" present. Here in the first place lies the reason for the theological importance which the question of the "real" presence of Christ in the sacrament of the altar acquired from the time of Berengarius of Tours.

There now took place in medieval times the opposite process—so to speak—to that which had occurred in the Eastern Church with the spread of the cult of icons. This, as we saw, started out from two real and authentic likenesses (or believed to be such) of Christ himself, in which it possessed the centre of a sacramental presence later extended to the likenesses of saints—the authenticity of which had also naturally to be established. It was just the opposite with Western Christianity, almost stifled under the weight of its relics: Christ had to be regained as the centre and made visible. Through the Eucharist, in the midst of the digressions of the cult of saints and relics, the centre of Christian faith was again given its proper importance. This occurred indeed in a way which remained completely in harmony with the long accepted habit of objectifying the faith in material substrates. All other aspects of the Christian faith came thus at first only into the background and had to be content on the theological plane with a tradition which did not really affect or form living devotion.

The fact that the meaning of Eucharistic devotion as it appeared to each individual grew out of the atmosphere of the habitual cult of relics and faith in miracles, explains also one of its aspects which can never be understood in purely theological terms. Eucharistic piety began at once, from the very beginning, to be shaped by the mentality of the age—that is, linked with an abundance of miracles centred on the Host or the precious Blood. Father Browe, in his book on this subject, has gathered together 200 such miracles and yet does not claim to have made a complete list.[19] For a theology which keeps in mind the liturgical reverence of the early Church and even more its sense of being evidently one with

62

the celebration of the mystery of the body and blood of our Lord, this trend cannot but appear to be a suspicious deviation. "The mystery to be understood gives way to the miracle which has to be believed" writes Père de Lubac and attributes the responsibility for this deviation to Scholastic dialectic, because it had changed "the notion of understanding itself".[20] By it the immediate interpretation of the understanding of faith had been replaced by distinctions of logical concepts and thus the great mass of the people—unable to follow these distinctions—could not but lapse into a state of spiritual simplicity in which they helped themselves as well as they could.

If of course we look less to the development of theological ideas than to the historical process, we cannot ignore the fact that Eucharistic piety—even in dubious forms—represented an enormous advance. We must not measure this against the early Christian theology, but rather compare it with the devotion to relics which immediately preceded and continued alongside it. As opposed to that attitude, the Eucharist gives the central Christian belief its rightful place—admittedly, in the objectivity and material visibility of the sacraments, taking the form established by the cult of relics. Soon monstrances appeared as vessels for the custody of the body of our Lord, analogous to reliquaries. In relation to these elementary developments the theological interpretation in the new scholastic concepts is—historically speaking—merely secondary; the orientation of Eucharistic piety in accordance with the pure theological concepts comes still later. This could only be effective at all when the Reformation had made theology a preliminary test of faith, with the result however that the spontaneous roots of faith died out in the course of time. In the parts of Europe which remained Catholic this process did not penetrate so deeply, but only because a considerable element of the old popular piety—including the theologically dubious aspects—was able to persist through the restoration of the baroque period until after that of the Enlightenment and even up to the dawn of the technical age.

We must return to the Middle Ages. The objectifying of the Eucharist, as the doctrine of the seven sacraments was made more precise,[21] had the effect that in the other sacraments the "matter" began likewise to be emphasized as distinct from the liturgical act. Of this all that remained relevant to the administration of the sacrament was the "form", that is, the formula uttered by the minister (generally, therefore, the priest). We need not concern ourselves here with the fact that in both Penance and Matrimony we have sacraments in which the "matter" cannot be a thing. It is more important to notice that generally the "form" of the formula cannot be separated from the administration of the sacrament, but there is a single exception—the "sacrament of the altar". Here the "form" of the sacramental words effects not the administration of the sacrament, but its existence as such, the "transubstantiation" of the bread and wine into the Body and Blood of our Lord. Eating and drinking certainly belong to the liturgical act of the sacrifice of the Mass as always, but only on the part of the priest and even then as a kind of accessory to the already existing sacrament. The emphasis has shifted from the reception of the sacrament to its "presence": the fact that this continues as long as the sacrament is not consumed rendered possible the Eucharistic piety which created for itself in the course of the later Middle Ages suitable liturgical forms in the feast of Corpus Christi, the procession of the Blessed Sacrament, the "exposition" of the Blessed Sacrament—at first in the chalice and later visibly in the monstrance—and even in the Mass celebrated in the presence of the Blessed Sacrament.

Christian faith certainly reached here the limit of objectivization and we must not lose sight of the fact that in the presence of this "God" reserved in the late Gothic "Sacrament-house" and later in the tabernacle or exposed in the monstrance, the humanity both of the worshippers and the worshipped threatened to be dissolved in the adoration. In the later Middle Ages it was not unusual to call the sacred Host simply "God".[22] This over-simple outlook obscures the fact that it is not God directly who is present, but Jesus Christ, and that he too is not visible in his divine glory but is in the hidden form of a slave, of "flesh and blood". In this way the existential anchorage of a specifically Christian morality—the Christian consciousness of brotherhood with Christ—then very easily disappears. The moral consequence of this is that there is a demand for a spiritual following of Christ which, even in the Franciscan movement, threatens to become superficial: an emphasis on concrete imitations of the man Jesus. At a later date, therefore, Christian morality was not in fact able to produce a convincing opposition to the secularizing and humanizing morality of the Enlightenment.

Through the objective isolation of the God-Christ, paradoxically enough, the divine presence itself which appeared to be emphasized became neglected. There disappeared in fact—or, better, there could only be inadequately developed —the equally Christian consciousness of possibilities of a divine presence other than that presented for adoration in the Eucharist, above all, that which is assured to every Christian as the most intimate gift of the Holy Spirit. This presented to Western Christianity a much greater danger than a weakness in its morality, namely, the danger of impotence: for it was no longer seen from the aspect of an existential and supremely personal endeavour and thus could no longer give a credible account of itself. We might therefore describe the new Eucharistic piety as having overcome the all too commonplace familiarity and availability of the cult of relics by a deeper reverence, but in regard to the presence of God had not led—or not sufficiently led—to that more exalted familiarity which was assured to us in the Incarnation.

VI

The Impact of Celtic Monasticism

THE earthy attitude of primitive people towards the super-natural world persisted, as we have seen, even after their acceptance of Christianity. Both theological and mystical subtleties were lost on them; even the liturgy and the Christian halo which the Empire had taken on remained for them phenomena belonging to the periphery of existence and the formative influence of these on the ordinary life of both the masses and the nobility is generally overestimated. It was the Cluniac movement which first drew leaders and people to any large extent into a fuller Christian life, mainly as a result of the regular intercession for the dead; the great pilgrimages also to Santiago and Jerusalem had similar results. In this context there can scarcely be any question of a theological influence at all; this became a matter of deeper interest with more widespread effects among the people only through Luther and his successors at the Reformation.

In order to understand Western Christianity the most important thing in practice is to see where and how in the ordinary life of the people—earthy and little penetrated by the supernatural—a permanent bridge to the new Christian God was built. We saw that the cult of relics was a very important link in this process; now we must turn to the decisive impact which Irish and after it Anglo-Saxon monasticism had on the formation of the West. We are not here concerned simply with the well-known fact that in distant Ireland, which had never been a part of the Roman Empire, much of the ancient learning inherited by the Middle Ages was preserved during the stormy times of the barbarian invasions and handed on again by way of England to the Frankish empire. Important as this heritage was, it consisted mainly of a literary tradition at first accessible only to the few. The most authentic and typical gift of the Irish is of a different character and it affected the broad masses of the people now converted to Christianity. Just like the ancient heritage, it came from outside into the midst of the Frankish kingdom; but the Celts were not the bearers of a superior cultural tradition—they were a primitive people, almost of the same cultural level, which had absorbed Christian influences merely at an earlier stage and more completely. Precisely for that reason, the Celtic "outside influence" was able to become part of the warp and woof of Western Christianity.

It was the Irish monks who brought this Celtic influence to bear upon the formation of Europe, after they had succeeded in introducing Christianity into the ordinary life of the Irish clans. Unlike the Egyptian monks, they did not completely abandon the world, but merely remained a little apart from it, in order to provide an example of asceticism valid also for the rest. They continued to be in close contact with their own clans, which they wanted to form—like the tribes of Israel—into a people of God. The monks thought of themselves—so to speak—as its levitical superstructure. In his own circle, the abbot was the spiritual leader, just as the chieftain was the secular leader, and he "had to take on something of the personal character of the prophets in the midst of this unstable circle of princes, judges and high kings".[1] Since the abbots were able to claim a monopoly of spiritual authority, their prophetic office was more like that of the Old Testament than that which the bishops on the mainland—and, later, the popes—claimed to embody. For the institutional Church in the strict sense, with its episcopal constitution, never really penetrated to these parts. In the

Irish Church the bishop was always merely one of the monks, ordained for those sacramental functions which required episcopal office, but living in the monastery and remaining in other respects under the jurisdiction of the abbot. This situation was maintained also in the Anglo-Saxon Church and even in the Church as reformed by the Normans, at least to the extent that some English bishops were simultaneously abbots of a monastery which served them as a cathedral chapter.

The close association of the Irish and Scottish monks with a world to which they gave direction and guidance continued even when they evangelized the Anglo-Saxons and later when they undertook those astounding missionary journeys which brought them as far as Salzburg, St Gallen and Bobbio in northern Italy. Naturally, they were not dealing here with one of their own clans, but with Celtic remnants or even a foreign people: these they made Christian or, if Christianity was already established but still insecure, they undertook their pastoral welfare. By the very fact of their existence in the midst of such a people, still more or less pagan, they set up the permanent vision and challenge of a Christianity seriously lived out and preached through personal example. It is impossible to overestimate the influence in those dark ages of an asceticism experienced at close quarters or the bravery of unarmed individuals who wandered into unknown foreign lands and through endless forests, still untracked and swarming with wild beasts. But, in this respect, the monks appealed also to a primitive instinct of the Celts and Teutons, which in many was quite as powerful as the bond of the clan: the drive of the individual to make a name for himself by his deeds and his steadfastness in face of danger. Thus the Celtic monks, like many others who came later, may have had a contagious effect on some of those with whom they came into contact. But their historical achievement lay not so much in this sort of "seduction to the monastery" as in the fact that they were able from the monastery to bring the impact of an ascetic way of life to bear also on the world around them. This influence became more decisive for the culture and education of the broad masses in medieval times than the oft-praised literary and scholastic influence of the Benedictines.[2]

The ascetic aspect of the medieval Janus-head is therefore rooted in the effect of the missionary work of the Celtic and later of the Anglo-Saxon monks, formed after the same pattern. A limit was set to this influence by the fact that it cut too deeply into the roots of natural life to be endured for long. It was of course obvious from the beginning that the full monastic asceticism could not be imposed as a universal requirement. The Christian character of the world had to be made evident in the field of morality: the monks, therefore, were concerned to provide religious practices to accompany every moment of life and, with the aid of strict sanctions, to secure the observance of the moral law. The principles of this morality were found in the prescriptions of the Old Testament, in both the decalogue and the ritual laws. In another respect also the Old Testament pattern became important for the formation of the Middle Ages: it was probably through the efforts of the monks that the anointing of kings, for long regarded as a sacrament, acquired a new importance.

We have seen that the effect of asceticism on the world has inevitable limitations. The same is true of the focusing of life as a whole on secondary religious observances and moral requirements. The appeal to the Jewish ritual law, particularly on the important point of sexual morality, went too far; but it must also be observed that even the fundamental law of the decalogue, like any law, works restrictively and cannot produce morality but only prevent immorality. This is certainly no small matter, but it is not in itself the Christian "fulfilling of the law". What was to be done within the field marked out by prohibitions and commands could not be stated by any moral law: this concentration on morality brought out what was permitted, not what was ideally possible. Hence morality in the West remained far too long one-sidedly ascetic, for the unique example set before the people for a long time was the monastic life of asceticism and religious observances.

By analogy with the monastic rule, the Celtic monks tried to make the law a "rule of life" for Christians in the world. The means adopted to secure this was to project the monastic penitential discipline into the world. In the monastery to every infringement of the rule an appropriate and often quite severe penalty was attached. The moral law, too, could be brought under the same form of discipline and this then imposed on Christians living in the world and not under monastic rule. Evidently, this possibility was first realized among the pupils in monastic schools and other persons who for a time had freely submitted themselves to monastic discipline.[3] The Irish monks made use of the sacrament of Penance in this way and thus gave it the form and—in practice—the central importance which it has had since then in the Roman Church. It is significant that Columban so emphasized the Pauline warning about receiving the body and blood of our Lord unworthily as to make the altar into a tribunal and the reception of Holy Communion into a judgment;[4] in this way it was possible for the practice to arise of preceding—as of necessity—every admission to Communion by a submission to the judgment of the sacrament of Penance.

It must be remembered that the Irish penitential practice differed from that of both the modern and the early Church.[5] It can be distinguished from that of the early Church by three essential characteristics: in the first place, it extended generally to all sins, both great and small; secondly, it gave scope for more frequent confession; and, thirdly, it substituted for public proceedings under the direction of the bishop a private act under the direction at first of the monks and then of the priests. The Roman practice on the other hand— we can only deal with this here, although in early times it was neither the universal nor the unique form—the Roman practice from the third century had admitted to penance the capital cases, which had previously been excluded, of apostasy, murder and adultery; but it embraced only the sins which had become known through a public judgment and those submitted in private confession *voluntarily* undertaken. The implementation of penance was in any case public, since it involved a total or partial exclusion from church services; its consequences outside the ecclesiastical sphere—such as exclusion from conjugal life, military service and participation in festivals—were also particularly burdensome after the Empire and the Church had entered into close union.

When the time of penance was completed, the penitents were readmitted on Maundy Thursday, without further absolution, to Communion (in danger of death, Communion was always possible without completion of the penance). We can well imagine that the burden of public penance favoured the custom of postponing submission until the moment of death. This usage—or, better, abuse—was in any case destroyed at its roots by the new Irish practice of private penance, since the implementation of the penance could no longer directly interfere with one's very existence.

Private penance now covered all sins, even those which could previously be remitted without a public act and outside the sacrament, whether by a simple act of contrition, by prayer or deeds of humility and charity. To every conceivable infringement of divine law there was assigned a definite penance, in the form of a real punishment. These were worked out in the penitential books, each author attempting to grade the penalties according to his own estimate of the seriousness of the offence. These have been of lasting importance, in as much as the drawing up of a penitential tariff presupposed an exact differentiation of sins according to class and gravity. This objective, essential distinction of sins became established and was later supplemented—especially in the Jesuit practice—by a comprehensive casuistry of the circumstances.

Among the Franks the new practice was introduced by the wandering Irish monks and the Anglo-Saxons. It had become general already by the time of Charlemagne, whose cultural ambassador and advisor, Alcuin, expresses surprise and disapproval in a letter to the "Brethren in the Province of the Goths" (Septimania) that the laity there do not confess to the priests, apparently because they want to maintain the early Christian practice.[6] It now became impossible to avoid a conflict on this point. But it took the form of a discussion on the great variations in the penitential books and came to an end through the gradual abandonment of both public penance and the use of these books. In their place emerged the practice of private confession and submission to the discretion of the bishop or of the confessor in regard to the penance to be imposed.

From the beginning private confession had been an indispensable element of the Irish penitential practice, since sins which were not publicly known had to be brought to the priest who absolved so that he could impose a suitable penalty. The later opposition to the penitential books and to the discretion of the absolving priest naturally led to the imposition of milder penalties. Confession now came to the fore in the proceedings and began already to be regarded as an essential part of the work of satisfaction, although it was always firmly maintained that this alone was not sufficient to wipe out all the so-called temporal *punishment* for sin. The Lateran Council of 1215 made annual confession obligatory for the entire Roman Church: the emphasis was placed on the sacramental efficacy (*ex opere operato*) of the priestly absolution. For the penitent the burden of the sacrament was transferred from the penitential deed to the preliminary examination of conscience and act of contrition. But this departure from the Irish penitential practice in no way alters the fact that the latter had brought about an enormous transformation in the Christian life. The decalogue remained as the rule for life in the world and thus became central in Christian consciousness and its observance the main object of Christian activity: by remitting offences against it, Penance took on in practice the role, as Troeltsch has termed it, of the "basic sacrament".

This turning-point had serious consequences for the formation of Christians in the West. For Christendom in its early stages participation in the Eucharistic cult, and with it the sense of having a status in the redeemed people of God, was completely to the fore: this central place was now occupied by moral effort to fulfil the commandments. This in turn made easier the process, already mentioned, in which the Eucharist from being a common and normal act of worship became the object of a special devotion separated from the public celebration of the Mass. Moral effort tended naturally to concentrate on prescriptions relating to sexual behaviour; and where the implications of the sixth and ninth commandments were not sufficiently clear, the detailed requirements of Jewish ritual purity were brought in to supplement them. Thus matrimonial intercourse was forbidden under pain of grave sin in Lent, in the period before Christmas (often also as long as forty days), as well as all Saturdays and Ember Days. Even at other times, because of the possibility of inordinate desire, the sexual act was regarded as at least venially sinful: thus the effect of Christian pastoral care was for some time to create in this respect a feeling of man's ineradicable sinfulness, a feeling which made its mark also on the Reformation.

These observations are not intended to justify the very

natural reactions which, since the period of the Enlightenment, have completely transformed the moral climate and
given rise to the opposite danger of a more or less general
libertinism. What is needed is to keep our vision clear for the
lacunae in Western morality, which are so difficult to see and
to fill up just because they are concealed as much by moral
over-exertion as by the easy-going attitude of the libertine.
We must call attention briefly to three important points.

1. As a result of the legalistic emphasis, the idea of a positive shaping of morality was lost. The all-sufficient aim of
moral effort appeared to be to behave according to the rule,
that is, to avoid infringements of the commandments or to
practise the virtues which would secure their fulfilment. In
all this, the fact was forgotten, or at any rate thrust into the
background, that life is not at all a sum of individual acts,
but a complete process which, in the Christian understanding, must at all times be seen especially as the way to God
and accepted as such. In these circumstances, Augustine's
advice, *ama et fac quod vis*, made as little impression as
Rozanow's intuition, "We shall be punished hereafter according to our want of love".[7] For under the dictatorship of the
law, love might appear as the "proximate occasion of sin",
even as a "remedy for concupiscence", but scarcely as a
positive and personal duty both inside and outside marriage.
We have already pointed out that the essence of every rule
is to restrict: it delimits the sphere of what is to be avoided
from what is to be done, but it cannot establish a positive
responsibility. Behaviour according to the rule, therefore,
may become an excuse for ignoring the fact that tasks to be
accomplished are set before us at all. The field committed to
positive freedom then appears to be one left open to individual choice and libertinism finds a nest in the very centre
of the personal conduct of life. It then seems as if the task
of morality and moral teaching is to extend ever more widely
—with the aid of probabilism—the limits of the permissible.

This preoccupation as much as the fear of moral dangers (which are, in fact, always present) distracts attention from the possibilities of a given situation and makes a person deaf to the voice of both nature and the Holy Spirit.

2. In spite of earnest moral efforts, Western Christianity became more and more in danger of underestimating the real presuppositions and consequences even of the "permissible". Scholastic philosophy had indeed defended in principle an autonomy—at least in a relative sense—of the secular sphere; but it took centuries for this to become established, and even then in face of considerable opposition from the Church and only as a result of the secularization spread by the "Enlightenment". We need only recall the moral ostracism of Macchiavelli which dispensed successive generations from the obligation even of examining the facts which he had made clear, although they determined the *raison d'état*, not only in his time, but also in the great modern states. We may also observe the way in which the canonical prohibition of interest prevented the elaboration of a systematic monetary theory, but did not hinder the practice of usury for instance, on the part of Jews, who were not subject to Canon Law—or the development of legal devices to get round the prohibition.[8] The difficulties, too, are well known which confronted at the beginning the development of new methods in the fields both of natural science and of history. Any investigation of the often scarcely edifying facts had to be pursued under the severe handicap that the world was not supposed to be under the rule of inescapable objective laws, but to be a moral structure wholly orientated towards mankind or at any rate to be open to a moral interpretation. Today we have finally come to the opposite extreme, at which it is claimed that morality itself needs an ontological basis, in as much as it represents nothing but the recognition and practical assurance of man's place within the community and in a world of objective facts.

3. Concentration on a sum of moral efforts and a constant examination of conscience tended in practice to reverse the natural trend, not only of action but also of reflection, and to put in the first place the formation of one's own personality. This "separatism" of the person ended in his "absolutism".[9] The solid reality of the partners of human life—God, one's fellow-man and the world—dissolved in the abstractions of a moral account which very easily became a pure calculation of utility. It was then logical for the Spaniards of the "golden age" to become painfully aware that they lived in an empty world, while the rest of Europe was simultaneously trying to make a virtue of necessity in accepting the Cartesian reduction of the world to the ego. It was also a solution which necessarily included an extension of the field of moral activity again to a social and political Utopia, and this in turn laid bare the ego as a mere agent of the dialectical world-process or progress.

It was the excavations of the nineteenth century which first created such a distance between us and our own past that an appreciation of the limits of European morality became possible. As Goethe puts it:

> *Und so verleugnet ihr das Göttlichste,*
> *Wenn euch des Herzens Winke nichts bedeuten.*

"You belie that which is most divine, when the heart's speech means nothing to you." To be deaf to the warning inner voice in regard to one's own way of life can in the end have a more far-reaching effect than even very serious infringements of the moral law. We may look back over the long-continued moral struggle of Western Christianity in the light of knowledge gained from depth-psychology and observe that "a real ethos has disappeared behind a mass of moral precepts" and that in most cases there was a substitution of "the moral code for the truly ethical decision which is a free one".[10] Linked with this is the new discovery that man can be held responsible not only for conscious but also for unconscious decisions: a discovery, in fact, "which Christian theology has hitherto scarcely noticed and has not yet adequately developed".[11]

When these facts have been appreciated, we are still only at the beginning of our task. For the scenery of events remains, for the time being, cluttered up with the consequences of the past. Historically speaking, into the vacuum of crippled personal initiatives—initiatives, of course, in the sense of fully responsible undertakings and not merely attempts to gain profit or prestige—there has entered the irresistible automatism of the machine: first of all in the religious sphere, then in the political, afterwards in the economic and finally in the technical sphere. The supreme moral danger of our time may be the shape on the horizon of a man "who not only cannot think and act for himself, but can no longer even conceive the idea of self-determined behaviour".[12]

The monastic-ascetic-moral trend was on the whole outside the main stream of ecclesiastical life in later Antiquity and, when it attempted particularly to gain a dominant influence in the Eastern imperial Church, it was rejected by the Byzantine emperors. In the Celtic countries which had remained free from Rome—in Wales, Ireland and Scotland—it was able on the other hand to develop into an all-embracing, all pervasive ecclesiastical form which then spread after the fall of the Roman Empire in the West into the far less consolidated and christianized succession-states of the Anglo-Saxons and the Franks. Thus a new factor was introduced, one not arising from the Roman tradition and therefore not generally appreciated at its true value, not springing directly from the main stream of Christian history before this but entering into it from the north-western edge of Christendom. It was linked—indirectly indeed and across a gap in the course of history—above all with the Old Testament tradition, in which was reflected both the monastic impulse and the Celtic clannishness. The essential forms of Celtic Christianity corresponded to this tradition: the social initiative of the monks acting in the spirit of the prophets, the thorough ritualization and moral shaping of the life of the people, finally the prophetic-priestly anointing which gave to kingship its obligations and legitimacy. The later compromise between the Irish and the Roman form of the Church did not hinder, but even promoted the success of the new factor emerging from the Anglo-Saxons under the spiritual influence of Celtic monasticism to gain universal importance for the whole Church.

This extraordinarily important fact is far too often forgotten when we recall the success of the Roman Church over Celtic "customs"—for instance, the different form of tonsure and the diversity in calculating the date of Easter. Against this, we need to emphasize the way in which essentially Celtic trends, through the mediation of the Anglo-Saxons and Boniface, entered into the structure of Frankish and therefore of Western Christianity as a whole. It was only by the Church's anointing that the Carolingians became legitimate sovereigns, but Charlemagne went further and conceived this sovereignty as ecclesiastical and directly concerned with the salvation of the souls of his subjects. In this spirit, he even extended the existing Frankish judicature to include an ecclesiastical tribunal before which all his subjects were to appear and submit their ecclesiastical and moral lapses in a public trial. Some of his theologians and councils also expressed themselves at this time in favour of an official confession at least once a year.

Irish monasticism was in close contact with the world and actively entered into it with ascetic and moral demands. Together with this, there now appeared on the scene a type of Western monasticism very different from the primitive form. The fundamental distinction from the primitive Christian monasticism maintained in the Orthodox Church was not established by the first foundation of St Benedict. His rule, with the prominence given to Roman disciplinary regulations and the importance attached to bodily labour, did of course reveal trends which went far beyond a mere flight from the world. Nevertheless, early Benedictinism kept at a distance from secular events and outside the sphere of politics: the entry of Theodoric's chancellor, Cassiodorus, in old age into the monastery which he had founded, continuing to work at his task of collecting and sifting ancient literature, at first made no difference to this situation. It was only the mission to the Anglo-Saxons and their undertaking of intellectual and educational tasks within the Carolingian Empire which made the Benedictine Order into that cultural institution of the Middle Ages which is described at length in secular history. Both tasks brought the Benedictines into decisive competition and later even into co-operation with the Irish monks and their Anglo-Saxon and Frankish foundations. But even then a genuinely political influence on the people was exercised solely by the Celtic monks and later by Charlemagne's Christian Empire. It was only after the collapse of that empire, in the course of the reform movements of the tenth century, that a role in ecclesiastical politics fell naturally to the Benedictines. The real political heritage of the Celtic monks was only taken up on a grand scale by later Orders. These made monasticism into an advance-guard of the Church at the service of papal policy and thus realized to the full the possibilities opened up by the Investiture contest. From then onwards the regional episcopal government could be undermined and by-passed by action from the centre on the part of the Pope, the Orders and the ordinary faithful mobilized in support of these.

The fact that the great ecclesiastical reform of the eleventh century was carried out under monastic auspices was therefore decisive. The spiritual sword then taken up by popes from the monastery naturally turned out to be two-edged. Since monks could not but approach politics from the ascetic standpoint, it followed that any secular action which they initiated must—at least, in the course of time—have the effect of dissolving earthly institutions. It would of course be a mistake to regard this as the sole factor working in that direction, since institutions always contain within themselves the seeds of their own dissolution which only wait for the appropriate time to become virulent. But it must be admitted that the breakdown of the old Europe was hastened by the undertakings of a monastic spirituality and that Rosenstock-Huessy is not entirely wrong in ranging the European revolutions in a series as successors of the medieval "papal revolutions" effected with the assistance of the monks.[13] Nor was it a question of monastic patrol activity simply against the imperial front: the radical wing, above all, of the Franciscans could hinder even reforms which were possible in practice and actually planned by presenting uncompromising maximum demands—indeed, they might go so far as to oppose even papal plans.[14]

The dissolving influence above-mentioned could be concealed only as long as the more important existing secular institutions seemed to decide its scope and thus to impose limits to its inroads. The relation of the Irish monks to their clans as the "new Israel" was certainly meant to work in that direction. But it became clear that the earthly institutions could not in the long run hold out against the united attack from their inner corrosion and a transcendent criticism. Empire and clan had to give way at an early stage to the "papal revolution"; the feudal institutions and the power of the great families declined with the Enlightenment and the Industrial Revolution, both of which would have been inconceivable without the "abstract" contribution of Western Christianity. "It only seems as if reason and Christianity in their necessary protest against an arbitrary separation had been for centuries drawing simultaneously on a capital which suddenly disappears."[15]

In the nineteenth century it began to be clear that this "abstract" power had largely determined the great revolutionary changes of history, but that of itself it had not been able to give a new shape to a levelled-down and atomized human society. For this it would have been necessary to go beyond the ascetic and restrictive influences and to bring into play also initiatives of a secular character—which, after centuries of excessive demands by a transcendent criticism, were no longer available. For example, the Church had always supposed that the sex-instinct would remain for the great majority of men the strongest determining factor in life and had been able therefore to treat of matrimony mainly in comparison with virginity—thus diminishing its importance and regarding it superficially. In so doing, she had not anticipated that, as a result of the Enlightenment and the technical revolution, not only the moral ends but even the full realization of sexual potential might be questioned. The Church also had constantly denounced the craving for glory, but had not anticipated that, after the levelling down of the smaller communities which nourished it, Beelzebub would appear in the mass-society in the form of the demagogue.[16] The unanimity, too, of monks and people in dreaming of a better world did not allow for the fact that the dream would be realized in the form of an industrial world of technical perfection producing unheard-of wealth and that, precisely for this reason, the divinely willed contentment with modest surroundings would become superfluous and the ascetic appeal based on it incredible. In brief, the Church had overestimated partly the solidity and partly the constancy of created institutions. Thus paradoxically her contribution led in the end to a world not *more* but *less* Christian, and this "less" of Christianity was due to a "less" of worldliness.

VII

The Impact of the Spanish Battle for the Faith

JUST as one new character came to be imprinted on Europe from its Celtic fringe, so another was developed at a different outpost and also entered into the formation of Western Christianity. The struggle for the faith in the extreme north-west of Spain later took on a universal form—not, however, by way of the Empire but by way of the papal Crusade. The Christian imperial idea itself implied the obligation of a mission and of making war against the heathen; but this struggle for the faith was different in two respects. Firstly, there was no question of conversion or incorporation into the Christian world, but of defence—primarily against Islam, but also against the internal enemy of the faith, the heretic. Secondly, the champions of the faith were called as individuals to a personal commitment and endowed with a religious character, while the war of the Empire against the pagans was waged simply by the army, in this respect doing no more than fulfil its political and Christian duty.

On the other hand, there were close links with Islam's "holy war" which, with its professional, ascetic fighters, provided in advance a model for the Christian Orders of chivalry. The Christian war of faith could never become like Islam's, a matter of divine law, but this meant little in an age given to theocratic ideas long after the theoretical distinction between the "spiritual" and the "secular" had been worked out in the Investiture contest. Nor did the character of the Islamic holy war as offensive and in principle aiming at world domination present much difference in practice from the Christian defensive action which, as a reconquest, was turned into an offensive in both Spain and Palestine. There was even a kind of exchange of starting-points, since Islam's holy war had already declined into a series of occasional forays.

The special character of the struggle for the faith arose out of concrete circumstances and a particular occasion—the Islamic conquest of Visigothic Spain in 711—but they were such as to lead to continuous warfare in defence of Christianity over a long period of time. The more or less casual Arab advance—which, contrary to all expectation, was successful—after the decisive blow against the Visigoths, followed a north-easterly direction prescribed by nature and policy towards the Pyrenees, at once a barrier and a point of contact between that country and the rest of the continent. By 721 the Arabs had the Pyrenees behind them and attacked Toulouse; in 732 they were thrown back from Poitiers by Charles Martel; but they continued until 759 the struggle with the Franks of Languedoc (*Septimania*) and from 778 again south of the Pyrenees against Charlemagne's offensive.

Under these circumstances, the north-western corner of Spain remained untouched by the Arab invasions and was at first of secondary importance in the conflict. Here at the "end of the earth" (Cape Finisterre), cut off from the rest of Christendom, a new Gothic remnant-state was built up through the initiative of Goths who had taken refuge there. It had to struggle hard for its existence, frequently changed its capital, but was saved as a result of two factors: about 740 the Arabs were held back by a revolution in Morocco which continued for two generations; and in 756 the foundation of a dynasty by the Umayyads—who had been displaced by the Abbasids in the last of the palace revolutions—led to their political separation from the rest of Islam. For some time, therefore, the Arabs had enough to do to keep up their defence against the Franks and were not capable of mounting a sweeping offensive in addition to this in another field—the Asturias.

Nevertheless, the people in those parts became accustomed to a continuous state of petty warfare: it had been kept up for a hundred years when Charlemagne died, and then—as a result of the weakening of the Frankish kingdom and consequently of the Pyrenean front—again took on a more serious aspect. The Asturian Christians had not much ground to lose. Their whole state and basis of operations consisted of a stretch of land 30 to 90 miles wide; it was indeed protected to a certain extent by the Cantabrian mountains, but this advantage was offset by the fact that it was soon threatened from behind by the Normans, who were disturbing and ravaging not only the Atlantic coast, but also the Iberian peninsula as far as Lisbon and Seville. In these decades of utter insecurity, having to defend themselves on all sides, the Asturian Christians found a symbol and a centre for their determined resistance, the importance of which for Spanish and European history as a whole has been recalled by Americo Castro in an informative if controversial book on Spain.[1]

The story was told later that in the year 843, on the eve of the battle of Clavijo, St James had revealed himself as the apostle of Spain and, on the following day had intervened as its champion, riding on a white horse and carrying a white banner. Some time before, his grave had been discovered in the ruins of the Roman city of Iria and his body was then solemnly transferred to its shrine in the neighbouring Compostela, which received its name from the "field of stars" (*campus-stella*), the Milky Way, where he was supposed to have appeared in the heavens. It may, incidentally, be recalled that the victories achieved by the Roman Dioscuri, Castor and Pollux, have been fused in this legend with those of the biblical apostles, James the Greater and James the Less. But it is important to note that James as the "brother of the Lord" could claim an authority comparable not only to that of Peter, Prince of the Apostles, but even to that of Christ. Since the body of Christ was no longer in the tomb, but had ascended into heaven, the body of his nearest relative in that relic-hungry age was—so to speak—the greatest possible pledge that could be given to a Christendom engaged in a hard struggle for existence on this earth. This fact alone made Santiago immediately into a centre of the Christian world competing with Rome, Aachen and Jerusalem; and as soon as the road from the Pyrenees was free again, it became the leading goal of pilgrimage—a kind of Christian counterpart of the Moslem Mecca.

It is not sufficiently realized that the crusades are to be understood, among other things, against the background of this veneration of St James and pilgrimages to his shrine. It must therefore be regarded as one of the essential factors in the spiritual and political ascendancy of the popes that they were able for a time at least through their wars for the liberation of the Holy Sepulchre to outbid both the pilgrimage to St James—which led to a cul-de-sac at the end of the world —and the Spanish battle for the faith—which, until then, had been of merely local importance.

In the ninth century, of course, when Asturias, beset on all sides in its narrow space, was struggling for mere existence, there was scarcely any question of the universal importance of St James. The saint and the veneration of his tomb served rather as a kind of guarantee of the endurance of Asturian Christendom in a continuous struggle under nearly impossible conditions. Castro has shown convincingly how this struggle for existence in a spirit of exaltation led to the emergence of a new type of Spaniard: the champion of the faith living in a world of illusory feelings and ideas. That in any event the basic image of St James as the Moor-killer (*Santiago Matamoros*) remained dominant for a long time, is shown by the Castilian legend of the intervention of St James and Aemilian on behalf of Count Fernan Gonzalez at the battle of Simancas a hundred years later (939); the only difference is that the ambitious counts, for reasons of prestige, associated the local saint—Milán—with James. But the later European success of the basic image becomes clear even in the eighteenth century, when the Turkish wars had lost most of their importance: for instance, in the Bavarian representations of the battle of Clavijo by the great baroque masters, Asam and Zimmermann.[2]

This western extension of the new way of faith and of life was brought about by the fact that Spanish Christendom from the beginning conceived its struggle for existence against Islam as a matter of importance to the whole Christian world. Death in the wars of faith was assimilated to martyrdom, a somewhat dubious procedure from the theological standpoint;[3] but martyrdom was quite exceptional at this time and therefore the defenders of the faith in practice inherited the glory and the exemplary character which in the early Church had belonged to the martyrs. Above all their idea of the central importance of the struggle for the faith found expression in the assumption of the title of the supreme Christian office by the champions of Spanish Christendom.

In 917 (after the disappearance of the Carolingian Empire), the deceased King Alphonsus III was described as *magnus imperator*; the kings of Leon and Castile who succeeded him bore the imperial title for more than two hundred years, and the attempt of Alphonsus X to gain the imperial crown after the end of the Hohenstaufen dynasty must be considered in this context. For the bishops of Santiago, the papal title of *pontifex*—later also of *apostolicus*—is found in documents from the year 954; the title was maintained until long after the Investiture contest, into the twelfth century. Naturally, it would be wrong to consider this as an actual leadership of all Christendom cast into juridical form, although our way of thinking today might lead us to do so: a tiny corner of Spain, caught up in a constant struggle for existence, had not the power even to attempt anything of this kind. But we must also avoid the mistake of giving these events a merely local significance, for they are undoubtedly an expression of the exalted mood of self-confident champions and of their consciousness of the unique and central importance of a new way of Christian living.

When this isolated defensive action was transformed by the support of all Europe into an offensive—the *Reconquista* —and Cluniac and Cistercian monks, knight-crusaders, peasant-settlers and masses of pilgrims re-established the sociological and intellectual contact of Spanish Christendom with the rest of the continent, they accepted the new Spanish imprint in spite of the attainment of hierarchical and liturgical unity with the Roman Church. The reason for this can easily be seen in the fact that the wars of faith in Spain remained necessary for centuries afterwards. At most, in these rather less dangerous times, the original mood of exaltation was softened and more widely spread, in as much as the warlike Santiago Matamoros took on a secondary, more peaceful character as patron of pilgrims and immigrants. On the other hand, thanks to the initiative of the popes and the propaganda of St Bernard of Clairvaux for the Second Crusade (1147-1149), the battle of the faith had in the meantime become a feature of the Church as a whole in the form of the Crusades and the Orders of chivalry.

For the war of faith so extended there was of course no longer a mobilization of whole peoples—as at the time of the Asturian-Moorish wars—but only of voluntary participants, the number of which however was considerable. But the fact that the Emperor Frederick Barbarossa took over the leadership of the Third Crusade, admittedly at a late stage and without permanent success, shows that the Empire as such was seeking to adopt this form. In this connection we may point to one of the gold-plated reliefs which adorn the shrine of Charlemagne at Aachen (1215). In the midst of the stars, the apostle James appears before the sleeping Charlemagne and promises him the possession of Galicia;[4] and on the right side of the relief the Emperor looks expectantly towards the Milky Way. The historical Charlemagne had no interest in occupying Galicia: his Spanish expeditions led him towards the valley of the Ebro. The late association with St James can be explained therefore only by the desire of the Hohenstaufens to attribute retrospectively to Charlemagne, as the ancestor who sanctions their empire (incidentally, after the French pattern), the legacy of the Leonine emperors and thus the role of a champion in the wars of faith: in this way, Charlemagne would have been the first crusader—long before the popes mobilized Europe for the First Crusade.

As a result of the danger from Islam, for the first time since the triumph of the Church under Constantine, the old idea of the *ecclesia militans* began to exercise a dominant influence on the course of history. It thus became possible to draw parallels between the martyr and the warrior for the faith, and for the latter to become a kind of representative of Christendom as a whole. Even if we disregard the dubious theology involved in this analogy, we must still keep in mind the grave historical problems which resulted from the prominence given to the battle of the faith and the type of Christian formed by it, just as they resulted in early Christian times from the importance attached to martyrdom. Both are certainly typical, but extreme situations which must be regarded historically as exceptional in the Christian life, being required at particular times and in particular regions.

In a general way, of course, just as the Christian must be prepared for martyrdom, so he must be prepared to fight for the faith; but he must not be required to take up permanently the attitude of a warrior for the faith. To take the war of faith as a normal situation of Christianity would cut off in advance any possibility of adaptation to the world and to historical events, and therefore also the possibilities of the existentially necessary association with non-Christians or with heretical Christians, of the presentation of Christianity itself to the world or even of a mission of reconciliation. In fact, later on Spanish soil, the commitment in principle to a fighting faith created the type of intransigence which, under the "Catholic Kings" (Ferdinand and Isabella) and the Hapsburgs, finally came to prevail as the norm. It led to the banishment of the Jews and Moors, but also made Spain itself for a long time incapable of making a fruitful contribution either to the course of history or to the growth of the European spirit. It is significant that the sole Spanish figure at this time of European stature, the great exception, Goya, is—among other things—an indictment of the type of the warrior for the faith.

We must not forget, however, that, before the time of the "Catholic Kings", the Spanish war of faith had led indeed to the *Reconquista* and thus to the overthrow by the Christians of Moorish domination, but not to a general christianization of the Moors and of the equally numerous Jews. The uniqueness and strangeness of the part of Spain in European history lies precisely in the fact that, at least throughout the Middle Ages, the equivalence of *imperium* and *ecclesia*, self-evident to the rest of Europe, never gained ground there—at least not outside the governing classes. The population of Spain, before and after the *Reconquista*, consisted of Christians, Jews and Moslems. All these groups, in principle good-naturedly tolerating one another, lived at first in regions ruled by the Moors and, after the reconquest had penetrated Moorish territory, in Christian kingdoms. To this extent the Spanish war of faith had ended merely in a vacuum. It had indeed secured the existence of the Christian remnant and given it political dominion over nearly half the peninsula, but otherwise it had led only to the co-existence of the three faiths.

Co-existence, however, brought with it not only legal tolerance but also cultural interpenetration. And although they were politically dominant, this factor worked out largely to the disadvantage of the Christians: the Moors were culturally superior and more advanced; Christianity had at its disposal moral and ascetic resources, but lacked initiative and formative power in the cultural sphere. Thus the Moors in Christian regions were able to set up not only the superstructure of their philosophy and art, but also the elementary refinements of civilized life—from underwear to chivalrous, polite behaviour. Both aspects, incidentally, became the basis of the whole European cultural advance by way of Christian Spain, the knighthood of Provence and Parisian scholasticism.

It became clear that the moral discipline of the West did not at all bar the way to this progress, since culture—as long as axioms of faith or morals were not questioned—could be regarded as "indifferent", a free sphere of "permitted" things. In fact, even under the one-sided moral presuppositions of Christianity, the more decisive questions of Christian cultural penetration or representation were not raised: among the great poets, Wolfram von Eschenbach was the only one who came near to doing so. Thus it came about that, while the comforts of life and aesthetics were regarded as of the highest importance in the knightly culture, dialectical ingenuity took first place in the world of learning. But all this could be taken over from the Moors without further examination and this cultural assimilation created in the late Middle Ages a community of interest between Islam and Christianity first realized in Spain, but of which the crusaders also were constantly made aware.

The climate of this cultural upsurge very soon gave way to an orthodox reaction, less speedily however in those Christian regions where Scholasticism successfully continued to demand at least in principle a "relative" autonomy for the secular spheres of culture. But in Spain, even at a time when tolerance still ruled between the different faiths, within the religious groups the stifling atmosphere of a life dominated by the Inquisition grew more oppressive. When reproaches are levelled at the Christian Inquisition, it should also be recalled that the famous philosopher Averroes was banished by the Moorish Inquisition and ended his life in a Jewish town near Córdoba, while the Jew Maimonides on the other hand went to Saladin's court to seek freedom for his advanced thought. But it is also worth noting that the Church entrusted the Inquisition set up against the Albigensians to an Order founded by a Spaniard, the Dominicans. When the "Catholic Kings" in the course of their policy of subordinating the Church to the State also made the Inquisition into a national institution, tolerance was abandoned in Spain and Jews and Moors were driven out—later, even those of Moorish descent. With the advent of the Reformation and the rise of three Confessional fronts, Spain undertook the leadership of the Catholic "Counter-Reformation" and it was again a Spanish Order—the Society of Jesus—which formed its spiritual backbone.

The renewal of the war of faith on these Confessional fronts largely determined the character of post-Tridentine Catholicism and left its imprint even on the "political Catholicism" of the nineteenth century. On the Protestant side a similar effect was produced especially by militant Calvinism in the spirit of the Old Testament, active in the Huguenot wars, the Dutch liberation and the "glorious" English revolution. But the wars of religion and—after the period of the Enlightenment—also the battles of the creeds finally ran into a vacuum. On the whole, they secured the defence of the Christian confession which happened at a particular stage to be in danger, but it was no longer possible on this basis to re-establish the lost unity and universality of Western Christianity. Moreover, the Christianity of the war of faith failed in the end to cope with the new requirements of political, economic and social co-existence which a completely new age brought with it.

VIII

Medieval Christianity

The Separation of Spiritual and Secular

MEDIEVAL Christianity took on its final shape in the course of the process of reform within the Roman Church and of the controversies between the Church thus reformed and the Empire. The outstanding feature of these events was that the papacy succeeded in gathering together under its leadership in permanent institutional form whatever was available of the elements which had gone into the making of historical Christianity. The Christian world-system which emerged in this way seems at first sight to be distinguished from the previous system of the imperial Church merely by the fact that the headship was transferred from the Emperor to the Pope. A closer examination, however, shows that the change went deeper—although it seems at first to have been concealed by the attempt to establish a papal theocracy.

The appearance is deceptive: the papal theocracy was not a closed system like that of Constantine, but one that could not remain unaffected by the great historical breach in its structure made through the reform of the Roman Church and in the long run leading to its breakdown. For all later history the decisive fact was that, at an early stage, at the height of the Investiture contest, European scholarship had worked out the conceptual distinction between the spiritual and the secular. For Western history and Western Christianity, on the other hand, the decisive fact was that their basic outlines had been laid down already before this distinction was established and therefore could be modified by it only to a very inadequate degree. The result of the great turning-point of history thus remained to a large extent theoretical, while Western practice continued to struggle with the problems of a world-situation already obsolete in principle.

The movement of ecclesiastical reform in the tenth and eleventh centuries arose—as historical research has adequately established—in the first place, not from an ecclesiastical or secular political programme, but from abuses which the unity of *imperium* and *ecclesia* brought with it for the spiritual life of the monasteries. The status of *Eigenkirche*, belonging to an ecclesiastical estate—that is, the fact that in Germanic law, like every other form of land-ownership, the church and its properties belonged to the domestic possessions of a noble family or of the king—carried with it the disposal of the personnel belonging to the estate, that is, the disposal of ecclesiastical offices. Juridical fictions, such as for instance the institution of lay-abbots, facilitated also an almost complete alienation of the estates themselves from their proper purpose, while the income of the monks or holders of ecclesiastical office was cut to the utmost. Even where the disposal of offices remained within "normal" limits, the secular obligations imposed on the ecclesiastical estate—provision of hospitality, payments in kind and military service—were so burdensome to the spiritual life of the monasteries and episcopal churches that reform became an urgent necessity.

It soon became clear, of course, that any attempt to produce a practical remedy for these abuses could not fail to come up very quickly against questions of principle and lead in the end to a revolutionary change in the whole social and political outlook. For this way of thinking was based on the identification of Empire and Church inherited from Constantine—their provinces were to a certain extent, but by no means completely, differentiated. This ancient heritage was given an even more drastically simplified expression in the

Western world in the form of *Eigenkirche* or "private church". The identification naturally persisted not only in the parts directly under the Emperor in the Middle Ages, but also in the Western kingdoms no longer under an effective imperial sovereignty. But it affected the Empire to a greater extent, since Otto the Great still appealed to the idea of the high-priesthood of the Old Testament in order to claim the rights of a priest-king over the dioceses and abbeys of the Empire.[1] Any energetic counter measures on the part of the Church in Germany would have been bound to bring about immediately a grave political crisis. From this standpoint also, it thus became clear that a satisfactory solution of the questions arising out of the Investiture contest was quite impossible.[2] An "honourable" solution would have required the practical implementation of the distinction between the concepts of spiritual and secular worked out by the canonists, above all, by Ivo of Chartres in 1100. The Emperor would then have left to the Pope the ordering of spiritual matters and therefore also the nomination of ecclesiastical office-holders, but on the other hand the Church would have had to restore to the Empire all the political power and possessions which she had gained from that source.

An attempt at such a radical solution was in fact made in the year 1111 by the Emperor Henry V and Pope Paschal II. Whether Henry's suggestion of a compromise was seriously meant or whether he allowed for the opposition of his bishops, is irrelevant here. The suggestion and its fate were bound, in any event, to reveal the actual situation. It failed because the German princes of the Church refused outright to give up their "secular" possessions, knowing that they would thereby have forfeited both their political power and their ecclesiastical independence of the Pope. After that, a solution of the conflict in principle was no longer possible; there could only be a compromise—and this was in fact achieved by the Concordat of Worms in 1122, the first of its kind. Here the academic formula of the separation of spiritual and secular was adopted and thus recognized as binding. Actually the dispute was settled on the earlier, territorial basis: in Italy the Emperor handed over to the Pope his power to settle the affairs of the imperial Church; in Germany he retained the power, in the legal form of a papal privilege. In European history, therefore, the solution took on a dual form: firstly, various modes of expression were found to sanction the union of the spiritual and the secular; secondly, the way was laid wide open for the formation of national Churches. The papal, "universal" Church was in fact predominantly Italian, with a majority of Italian cardinals in the Curia even up to the present time.

While appreciating these problems, we must not go to the other extreme and suppose that an absolutely uncompromising and "pure" separation of the spiritual and secular is in any way an historical possibility. Even a Church keeping strictly to its spiritual mission would have to be able to call its own at least such worldly possessions or income as were necessary to secure the exercise of its functions; and there would always be some discussion about the extent of those functions, the way in which they might be secured and the means necessary for this. In principle, it must be noted that possessions extending beyond a certain limit—which is hard to define—become "wealth" in the proper sense of the word; thus, they not only occasionally go beyond what is necessary for the exercise of spiritual functions, but also become a specifically political power. For instance, the fact that the clergy of Mainz at the time of the Reformation owned— free of tax—a third of all the dwelling houses, cannot be considered merely from the point of view of spiritual necessity.[3]

Since the Church's possessions have a certain natural growth, their recognition in principle carries with it *eo ipso* the historical necessity of imposing restraint from time to time in the light also of secular interests. To that extent, Charles Martel's secularization of ecclesiastical property, as Western Europe was beginning to take shape, is a typical instance: in urgent cases of public need or even of a disturbance of public order, such an act cannot be regarded without qualification as sacrilege and all that can be required or negotiated is the guarantee of secular claims indispensable to the normal exercise of ecclesiastical functions—which is what happened in the end on that occasion.

It is characteristic of the Roman ecclesiastical reform that it appealed beyond the imperial Church to the past and to the "early Church". Thus the distinction between spiritual and secular worked out by scholars could be linked with the letter of Pope Gelasius to the Emperor Anastasius (494), in which two tribunals are described as authorized to rule *this world* (*hic mundus regitur*): the sacred authority of the *pontifices* (*auctoritas* was the term used of the Roman senate, not to be translated—as it often is—by "power") and the royal power, which is not qualified by a religious predicate. When Gregory VII drew the logical conclusions from this tradition and disputed the Emperor's right to deal with the affairs of the Church, the Constantinian unity of *imperium* and *ecclesia* was dissolved in principle. Accordingly, in the West, the Church kept the predicate of "holy" and the Empire lost it.

In Byzantium a final and unbridgeable cleavage had been created, as long as there remained an imperial dynasty— either on the spot or in its successors in Russia—which considered itself, its functions and its symbols to be holy. But the Empire of the West, even when placed by Otto the Great under an Old Testament high-priesthood, was in principle deprived of its sacred character and the Emperor himself laicized. The German language conceals this process by rendering the Latin *sacrum* as well as *sanctum* as "*heilig* (holy)". Thus, when Barbarossa added *sacrum* to the imperial title, *imperium romanum*, the whole was translated as "the holy Roman Empire". It is, however, significant that the Hohenstaufen reaction to the new situation created by Gregory VII could no longer go so far as to claim for the Empire the title of *sanctum*. Instead, Barbarossa, following the example of other kings, had to assert that Christian holiness was mediated to the Empire through the canonization of Charlemagne; Frederick II went a step further and interpreted *sacrum* to mean the immediacy of God to the Empire, by a direct appeal to the notion of cult implied in the pagan-Roman *justitia*.

In both the title and the phraseology of the Concordat of Worms, the "separation of the spheres" prevailed. But we have already observed that this was not the case in political practice, or at least only partially. The compromise of the Concordat of Worms was settled on a territorial basis, in as much as in Germany the imperial tradition was maintained and in Italy on the other hand abandoned. This settlement, therefore, already anticipated the end of an imperial power essentially based on the right to dispose of bishoprics. When the Hohenstaufens attempted to set up afresh the imperial sovereignty in Italy, in a roundabout way with the aid of Roman Law and Norman State practice, they came up against the determination of the popes to resist to the bitter end, to maintain under all circumstances the states of the Church and ecclesiastical rule over all Italy. On the other hand, the attempt of the popes to extend their success also to Germany met with the firm resistance of the awakening German "nation". It was not the Pope, but the princes who gained here what the Hohenstaufens had lost, and the Reformation set its seal on the situation of a regional ruler exercising authority over the Church in Protestant areas and also more or less in those which remained Catholic. After the breakdown of the attempt at papal theocracy, this was also the normal situation for nations as a whole outside the German lands in Europe, either in a loose association with the central

Roman government as in France and Spain or through breaking away from this association as in England and Scandinavia.

It was in the Investiture controversy that,* for the first time, scholars openly asserted their right to be consulted in the great problems facing the Christian West and even imposed their formula for solving these; but in the circumstances, they had to be content with a moral success and to go forward under the protection of the power which happened at the time to be victorious. They were able, indeed, to secure their first position as auxiliaries to the reforming Church with the aid of scholastic philosophy based on a complete acceptance of Aristotle and therefore upholding in principle the autonomy of the secular spheres of activity (philosophy, politics, economics, art); the permanent association of these with the spiritual sphere they saw as assured in advance through their immanent, teleological orientation as "created orders". But the university failed in its attempt—which was easy to understand—with the aid of the conciliar movement, at the time of the Great Schism, to gain the supremacy over the government of the Church. Since this attempt, which was warded off only with the greatest difficulty, the Roman central government has regarded its one-time auxiliary with a marked reserve and until well into the

---

* The dispute dating from the close of the eleventh century and the beginning of the twelfth over the claim of the Emperor and other lay princes to invest an abbot-elect or bishop-elect with the ring and staff and to receive homage before his consecration. The custom was condemned by Pope Nicholas II in 1059. Gregory VII forbade all lay investiture in 1075. In later years, with attempts to enforce this legislation, wider political issues became involved. A formal settlement reached by the Concordat of Worms in 1122 was reaffirmed by the Second Lateran Council a year later. In Germany the Emperor relinquished his right to invest with ring and staff, but continued to bestow temporalities and to receive homage as well as being allowed a say in elections. In England the dispute centred on St Anselm, Archbishop of Canterbury, and Henry I, the former refusing to do homage or to consecrate bishops who had received lay investiture. In 1107 the Council of London ratified a compromise which permitted Henry to receive homage and grant investiture of temporalities before consecration. In return he guaranteed freedom of election.

nineteenth century suspected rather than promoted the development of effective scientific methods. It was under Protestant influences that this took place; and it was in Protestant circles that theology, from the beginning of the Reformation, secured an unmistakable right to be heard even as against the local ruler's claim to govern the Church.

Because concrete scientific methods in secular fields on the whole were developed only at a later date, the scholastic recognition of these in principle remained at first merely a framework—even for intellectual activity—which would need revision in the light of actual advances in knowledge. Purely traditional Scholasticism, therefore, very soon became entangled in a proof-mechanism of logical subtleties and—in contradiction to its own principles—was inclined to deal with secular problems as secondary and predominantly from the theological standpoint (hence the bitter opposition, for instance, to the claim of natural science that the earth is not the centre of the universe). Our comments on the unsuitability of the Greek conceptual structure for grasping the basic human and divine relationships—which cannot be reduced to "objects"—may also be applied to a Scholasticism based wholly on Aristotle. At the same time, even a modern philosophy will only neglect the abundance of traditional material freshly elaborated in medieval Scholasticism to its own disadvantage. It must also be recognized that this at its best first embodied that pioneer achievement which has since been the prerogative of science in the fabric of Western life and society. This achievement rests on the fact that, through the separation of the spiritual and the secular, the first distinction in principle came to prevail against a spiritual and political unity which, although now obsolete from the intellectual standpoint, continued for centuries to dominate European life in practice and found in modern times a very anachronistic resurrection in the secularized form of the totalitarian State.

A Church which upheld the distinction of spiritual and secular in its relations with the Empire could not simply describe its own sphere as "holy" and leave it at that. Since it claimed to be a visible Church on earth, it had to recognize the distinction as applicable to itself and separate within its own life the *sanctum* from the earthly element. This necessity brought with it the further need to shift the emphasis away from the personal and communal to the institutional aspect. The early Church had regarded itself predominantly as the reality which we are accustomed to call today the *corpus mysticum*, that is, as the community of Christians with the saints already in glory and with Christ their head. But in such a personal conception the distinction of spiritual and secular could be made only with great reservations, for the Church on earth included both just and sinners, who were scarcely distinguishable from one another; and even after death, in another world, the fate of individual Christians was by no means clear. In any case, only a small number of these could be regarded with any certainty as saints and it is significant that about the year 1000 the new form of "canonization" begins to prevail as the juridical prerequisite for their public cult.[4]

A strict division, therefore, could be maintained only in regard to the functions of the Church on earth. Thus about 1150 the doctrine of the seven sacraments as the proper field of the Church's holiness was established and the administration of these sacred functions determined the group of persons who primarily represented the Church, namely the clergy. From this standpoint it was a matter of indifference as to whether the minister of the sacrament was in a state of grace, or even at times whether he was properly a member of the Church: the sacrament had its effect *ex opere operato*, in virtue of the function exercised in accordance with the rules (*rite*) by the person authorized to do this—not in virtue of his personal sanctity. This turning-point meant in practice de-liturgizing the Church and simultaneously reducing it largely to the clerical element, to which normally the administration of the sacraments was committed. The emphasis was shifted therefore from the act of priest and people together to the formally correct execution of his functions by the priest.[5] The change found its expression in Canon Law, which began to be worked on afresh and modified in the twelfth and thirteenth centuries.

Even in regard to the sacraments themselves the emphasis was again shifted from the priest's administration to the means he used and to the object sanctified by his words in order to effect holiness: to the water, the oil, the bread for the Eucharist. In this "matter" of the sacraments there remained in the innermost centre of the Church a small relic of a sacred world in which the division of the secular from the spiritual found its term. At this limit, the Church opposed the far-reaching "rationalistic" attempts of Berengarius of Tours and of Abelard to reduce the administration of the sacraments to a mere symbol and to transform their reality into a purely "spiritual reception". The residue of an immediate divine presence was preserved. But along with this was the overwhelming part of the ecclesiastical functions and institutions which belonged to the "secular" side of the distinction—although, even here, the Church insisted on its competence and did not, for example, hand over the *jus circa sacra* to the political power which ruled over the secular sphere in the proper sense of the word.

The distinction admitted within the Church found its juridical expression in the juxtaposition of a divine law "instituted" by Christ and therefore immutable and a human, ecclesiastical law which might be changed. The divine law was restricted to the sacramental sphere and thus included the hierarchical order in the Church which was implicit in the sacrament of the priesthood. All the rest belonged to the sphere of the Church's man-made law, which was admitted to be changeable according to times and circumstances and was in fact completely transformed by the great ecclesiastical reform of those centuries.

It might now have been thought that the actual state of this human, ecclesiastical law—acknowledged to be "historical"—would also have demanded an historical justification: in other words, that the great turning-point of ecclesiastical reform would have been interpreted historically in the light of a comparison with the earlier state of the Church (*status ecclesiae*),[6] just as at the beginning the sacramental nature of the Church had found its justification in the history of salvation by a reference to the earlier state of salvation-history in the Old Testament. But this is just what did not happen, and it is, incidentally, an indication of a serious deficiency in the content of scholastic philosophy. The profound transformation of the *status* of the Church did not yet bring out a properly historical consciousness: indeed, even the old awareness of the distinction between the Old and the New Testament in the history of salvation—already losing much of its force under the overwhelming pressure of the moralistic approach—largely sank in the wake of historical unconsciousness.

The Church's law was justified one-sidedly solely *ex auctoritate*, that is, juridically: the divine, by the plenitude of power possessed by the divine Founder of the Church; the human, by the power delegated by the same divine Founder to the Pope. More far-reaching questions were not only not admitted to be theological: in practice, they were not even raised. This abandonment to "the will of the legislator" stabilized at the very centre of Western Christianity an almost unassailable sphere of positivism which spread thence into the political activities of the medieval Church and thus further to politics and society as a whole. It was an historical consequence of this filiation that the perfected and total positivism of the nineteenth century had such a relatively easy game against the defensive action of Western Christianity: the latter had itself bred and reared positivism.

Christendom

There remained, inevitably in this situation, an ambiguity which decisively influenced the development of Western Christianity. In theory, the Church adopted the distinction between spiritual and secular worked out in the Investiture controversy and in particular recognized its validity even in internal, ecclesiastical affairs. But in fact—and especially in the secular sphere—the old identification remained more or less in force. The only difference was that the Church put in place of the old concept of unity—the *ecclesia universalis*, embracing Empire and Church—the new, more secular concept of "Christendom" as a *corpus mixtum*. From the theoretical subordination of the secular to the spiritual Cardinal Humbert and Pope Gregory VII already drew the conclusion that in this *corpus mixtum* the Church as the superior factor not only held the first place, but had also the right of a final decision. From this point of view, no matter what formulas and stipulations were adopted, logically there was bound to emerge an attempt at papal theocracy, that is, an attempt to gain *spiritual* supremacy for the Church. The attempt included the more or less well-meant applications of spiritual means—such as censures and indulgences—to worldly ends and political means—such as the death-penalty or war against heretics—to spiritual ends.

In spite of the distinction in principle between divine and human law, the old coincidence of *imperium* and *ecclesia* persisted as a fact in a world now deprived of its sacred character and in theory, as profane, left to itself by the Church. We have already mentioned the logical attempt at a solution by the Emperor Henry V and Pope Paschal II, which was bound to fail in a world organized from pagan times in the light of the sacred character of rulers and of a universal public cult and taken over in this form by Constantine into the Christian era. The intervention of the reforming Church in this thousand year old world-structure and the readjustment to a new theory—although this, in the Christian view, was more correct—were not able to demolish in a moment the old system, still capable of putting up a strong resistance, and replace it by one more in accordance with the new ideas. Even when in the French Revolution the old structure really broke down, the erection of a new one remained an open question and remains so to the present day: the Church of the nineteenth century particularly made very great efforts to retain from the old, familiar positions whatever could be preserved.

At the height of the Middle Ages no one thought of abandoning entirely the Constantinian unification of Church, State membership and nationality. The "sects" at most played with the idea, but neither Pope nor Emperor could even imagine that State and people as a whole might not be and remain Christian. Baptism was—to adopt Heinrich Heine's somewhat irreverent expression, understandable enough as a result of the Church's entanglement in the whole world-situation—the ticket which alone secured admission also into the political and cultural sphere. Deviations from the Church's doctrine or serious infringements of her practice led without more ado also to civic discrimination or even "liquidation". Since now the Church had withdrawn from the imperial-ecclesiastical cosmos and formed itself into a special ecclesiastical sphere of a sacramental-clerical character with its own laws, the remaining sociological-political world could no longer be described by the old-familiar term "Church": the popes therefore adopted (Nicholas I in the first place) the new concept of *Christianitas*.[7] "Christendom" now meant what "Church" *tout court* had previously meant: the whole body of Christians in their ecclesiastical, political and social unity. The more restricted, special sphere of the sacramental-clerical Church was also incorporated into "Christendom" as a "visible" reality, united to it afterwards as before by a thousand traditional ties.

It was from this ambiguity that the Church's claim to political sovereignty emerged. This was logically justified by the higher rank of a Church which had to deal with divine and spiritual matters, but factually and historically it was a sociological self-misunderstanding, in as much as this pre-eminence with its transcendent justification and formation was "understood" as a social and political priority of *power*. The Church as a whole entered on to the same plane as all the other sociological groups, being merely the first of these. This "sociological self-misunderstanding", which thrust the transcendent element into the background and regarded it mainly as an auxiliary to secular activities, made the Church the first example of an attempt to establish a total sovereignty, since she had to try to incorporate all spheres and all the phenomena of life into the whole scheme of her norms and—of greater importance historically—legal sanctions.

Even after the failure of the papal attempt to gain world-sovereignty in 1300, this mentality persisted, living on after the upheaval of the Reformation in the Catholicism of the Counter-Reformation in the sixteenth and seventeenth centuries and again, after the breakdown of the feudal world, in the "political" Catholicism of the nineteenth century. It struck at the "sacramental reality" of the Church, since from the time of the struggles with the Hohenstaufens and particularly after the Avignon captivity concern for her political and financial security took precedence over all specifically ecclesiastical interests. Even the reconsideration of this at the Council of Trent did not fully succeed in bringing about the necessary change of emphasis because of the entanglement of the Church in secular affairs. Even the sacraments might seem at times—as Heine's reference to baptism shows —to be more a testimony of sociological attachment and of the privileges associated with this than a means of access to the transcendent reality embodied in them; in the nineteenth century, at any rate, this was the great danger involved in being a so-called "practising" Catholic.

Historically, the papal claim to full imperial power was asserted only for a relatively brief period in the thirteenth century—from Gregory IX to Boniface VIII (1227-1303). But, in spite of the relative brevity of the time, this is not to be dismissed as a mere episode. So much is clear from the simple fact—already mentioned—that the mentality created by it lasted up to the beginning of the twentieth century. For it is of no small importance from the standpoint of world-history in general and of German history in particular that the political destruction of the Hohenstaufen Frederick II by Popes Gregory IX and Innocent IV—the failure of the last great imperial venture of the Hohenstaufens as a result of papal action—should have occurred at this time : the consequences of these events have left their mark on Germany until the present day. Professor Kempf of the Gregorian University tried some time ago to evaluate the modest and conscientious attempt of Pope Innocent III to balance the mutually conflicting claims of Church and Empire by means of a comparison with the excessive efforts of these later popes.[8] His treatment of the subject deserves careful attention. He does not make the result of the conflict of Innocent's successors with Frederick II seem any the less tragic, but he does draw our attention to the complexity of the situation at that time and thus makes an important contribution to an understanding of the state of affairs today.

Kempf is at pains to clarify the notion of the papal plenitude of power (*plenitudo potestatis*), which was later invoked to establish the right of a papal theocracy and today is still generally understood in this sense. Undoubtedly the notion covers wholly and entirely the position which the Pope has claimed since the great ecclesiastical reform within the special sphere of the sacramental-clerical Church. But Innocent III, going beyond the ecclesiastical field in the narrower sense to the ordering of secular affairs, wanted to include in this concept what were to be understood as exceptional rights (*casualiter et certis causis inspectis*): he was not trying simply to justify the assumption of supreme political power, which belonged to the Emperor. It is a question of a summary of rights—in fact, limited rights—which Innocent regarded as indispensable for the security of the existence and mission of the Church, namely: (1) sovereignty over the states of the Church; (2) feudal sovereignty over the vassal-states of the papacy; (3) the right to be consulted on the election of an Emperor, since his position as advocate of the Church touched her more closely than the authority of other rulers; (4) a general power to intervene in the political sphere on moral grounds (*ratione peccati*).

The first three of the rights here claimed concerned the Emperor directly, because both the sovereignty of the Pope over the states of the Church and his feudal overlordship over the kingdom of Sicily were bound to prevent the union of Italy under imperial leadership. With the breakdown of the Hohenstaufen Empire and only a little later also of the papal theocracy, these rights claimed by the Pope were in fact abolished already in the fourteenth century, with the exception of that concerning the states of the Church—which was maintained in fact until 1870 and in law even until 1929. We may therefore be content to raise one point only, but this must be made more clear than it is in Kempf's book.

Exceptional constitutional rights under normal circumstances do not necessarily disturb seriously the ordinary course of events, but when the circumstances are such as to involve a conflict of principle they can always wear down in the long run the opposing claims and positions. In our own time, for instance, the whole Weimar Constitution in Germany was reduced to impotence because of the exceptional rights asserted in article 48.[9] In the thirteenth century also all these exceptional rights led to the downfall of the Emperor Frederick II, because the papal claims asserted in them were opposed to both the Italian policy of the Hohenstaufens and their efforts to make the imperial dignity hereditary in their own family. The popes went further and, by appealing to the *ratio peccati*, asserted successfully against the Emperor a large number of moral arguments, some of which were justified while others were not.

As far as the right of intervention *ratione peccati* is concerned, according to present-day ideas, there can be no doubt that the Church may both pass moral judgment on world-events and likewise impose ecclesiastical penalties on persons who are her subjects—and therefore on the holders of political office. But it must be observed that these rights in the age of "Christendom" had immediate political consequences. When the Pope delivered a moral judgment, he at once turned it into political counter-measures, and an ecclesiastical measure against the king affected not only himself as a member of the Church, but the very State over which he ruled as an institution. For, as a result of the reform, the Church was now completely objectivized and institutionalized in a clerical form; no other human association had yet been organized in the same way, with the exception of certain relatively small states founded by the Normans.

This "early start" in institutionalizing must be taken into account as a predominant factor in the development of the Church's power in the Middle Ages. A spiritual process against a ruler, no matter how well justified, meant at that time a direct attack with superior force on the State which still found its essential expression solely in his person. That is why not only the Hohenstaufen dynasty, but also Italy and the German Empire together were affected by the decisive struggle led by the Pope against Frederick II in a way which historically could not be repeated. A real purification of the intervention of the spiritual power *ratione peccati* from any semblance of encroachment was, therefore, possible only after the secular spheres had taken on an objective and institutional character analogous to that of the Church. Frederick II's Sicilian state seemed so dangerous to the popes precisely because its development was taking place in the closest proximity to the states of the Church.

The theocratic development of the papal plenitude of power presupposed a greatly weakened empire; in the East this did not come about before 1071 or even 1204. On the other hand, the Roman Empire had declined in the West already in the fifth century and in its place a number of Germanic local sovereignties had been set up, which Isidore of Seville already could conceive as a unity only by linking them together under the one Church.[10] In Clovis' kingdom moreover, by contrast with Theodoric's, religious allegiance was from the beginning the decisive factor and this emphasis on the Church could no longer be reduced to what it had been under Constantine, even when the theocratic unity of Church and Empire emerged in Carolingian times. And when, after the rapid dissolution of the Carolingian Empire, Otto the Great in 962 restored the prestige of the Western Emperor, he acted indeed as the lord of a mighty realm, but still of a particular area; for that very reason he tried to embellish this imperial dignity with memories of the Jewish high-priesthood.[11] In the ensuing test of power the Pope therefore was able to play off against the Emperor, not only internal German conflicts, but also national differences. "Who has made the Germans judges over the other nations?" was the question raised when Barbarossa tried once again to set up popes of his own choice. In this situation there seemed to be a prospect of success for an attempt to set up in place of the the imperial authority, which had become limited to a particular area, a truly universal political authority, attached to the universal power of the Church and if necessary making use of this to decide an issue.

Hence the clerical Church of the reform movement did not appear on the political plane so much in that form as in the role of heir to the vanquished Empire. The Constantinian title of representative or *vicar* of Christ was transferred to the Pope and the latter as supreme leader of Christendom now added to his spiritual power also a kind of super-imperial power. Thus, since the time of Gregory VII the popes have claimed also the imperial insignia, the most impressive of which is the tiara with the crown surrounding it (from the time of Innocent III there have been two crowns, from that of Boniface VIII three), significantly called *regnum* and still worn today—though only on solemn occasions other than church services.[12] Among the developments of the reform period are to be included, therefore, not only the vanquishing of the imperial Church by a spiritual appeal to the early Roman *status ecclesiae*, but also an express politicizing of the Church under papal leadership.

It is in this spiritual-secular dual burden that the ambiguity of the Church in her second millennium lies. The process of politicizing can be perceived from the time of Gregory VII in the so-called *dictatus papae*, in the alliance of the Church with the Normans, in the attempt to encircle the centre of Europe by a system of papal vassal-states, and finally in the efforts made to organize the states of the Church in a more rigidly feudal form and to extend them at the expense of the imperial lands in central Italy. It culminates in a series of "political popes" from Innocent III to Boniface VIII (1198-1303) and, after the breakdown of papal secular politics, fades out in the lesser forms of fiscalism, central Italian territorial policy and curial diplomacy.

We must not, however, lose sight of the fact that this ambiguity was only possible because "Christendom" was generally understood simply as the continuation of the old unity of Church and Empire. The secularization which actually set in through the distinction made between spiritual and secular was concealed by the fact that Christendom emerged in a way from an ecclesiastical leadership and was seen as a part of the tradition of the old sacred unity of Empire and Church. At the decisive moment, the Hohenstaufens almost alone saw that the reduction of the Church to a special field opened the way to the absolutely novel possibility of an autonomous development of state-institutions parallel to the Church. Their attempt to bring this about, particularly that of Frederick II, who for a long time was very circumspect in his procedure, was not really in opposition to the Church but only to her claim to absolute sovereignty also in "Christendom" and especially to her secular demands in regard to northern Italy and the states of the Church. This policy of the Hohenstaufens was taken up again, but much more forcefully, by France from about 1300 and has led to the formation of what we call "the modern State".

Complexio Oppositorum

If we survey the politicizing of the papacy in a larger context, we see that it represents only a part of a whole process directed by the new central government of the Roman Curia. This curial centre succeeded in shutting out other centres in the Church by taking over their characteristic forms, with their power to rouse the enthusiasm of the faithful, and binding these with Rome. In this connection there is a political—or, better, an ecclesiastico-political—activity which can be observed wherever the organization of a new Christendom centred on the Holy See appeared to have a prospect of success.[13] Apart from the imperial Church system, it is mainly the "modern" forms of the Irish and Spanish tradition which must be considered in this process of annexation. The new amalgam was worked up as a distinctive objective reality, based on the tradition of Germanic piety and in the end fitted out with a complete theory emerging from the upsurge of learning and renewing the old alliance of Christianity with philosophy, bringing Christian scholarship under the aegis of the Church.

1. The contribution of the Irish Church was a thorough moralizing of Christian life and the provision of a sanction in the institution of private penance. This contribution was taken over by Rome and, in the course of time, replaced the traditional public ecclesiastical penance, but with very important modifications. The association of private confession with a personal act of penance drawn from the tariff in the penitential books was abandoned and broken down into its parts, sacramental confession and non-sacramental personal penitential practices. The former soon ceased to appear merely as an unavoidable preliminary to the imposition of penance, and became itself an essential part of the work of satisfaction, so that the official penance gradually diminished and might be reduced finally to a token prayer. But, on the other hand, personal acts of penance of a very burdensome character were left to the free choice of individuals: some of these forms of self-mortification, which had hitherto seemed impracticable, were spread after the tenth century from the reformed monasteries in Italy. Shortly before the Investiture controversy, one of the pioneers of the new penitential practices, the reforming monk and cardinal, Peter Damian, had attacked in detail the penitential books with their tariff-schemes and thus—so to speak— "liberated" the penitential practices; simultaneously the reforming Pope, Alexander II, recognized the bishops as ultimate authorities in matters relating to the sacrament of Penance and thus left to them the decision as to the due amount and form of the official satisfaction. In practice, this led to a diminution of personal effort which was deplored by the rigorists, but which was on the other hand compensated by a climate favourable to freely chosen works of penance.

It is a matter of importance for later history that the primitive custom of vicarious satisfaction now developed in a unique fashion within the penitential system. It had already been possible within the tariff-scheme for someone other than the sinner to undertake the imposed penance in his place, so much so that a wealthy man might shift off his expiation, no matter how severe, to a number of paid substitutes. From this there developed in the eleventh century the ecclesiastical institution of indulgences[14]—oddly enough, in those parts which upheld the older Roman tradition and, as we saw, stubbornly resisted the new procedure of private penance, namely Southern France and Catalonia. Some bishops released people from public penance if they performed such easier tasks as almsgiving or making a visit to church. The popes, at first reluctantly, took up this new practice and thus set themselves up without further question as the final authority also for the Irish system of private penance. The first instances of papal action are the plenary indulgence granted by Alexander II in 1063 for the Spanish warriors and by Urban II in 1095 for the Crusaders. The standard was set here and practically for the whole development in the Church by the IV Lateran Council under Innocent III, with its decree on the crusades and its exemplary formula for alms-collections; the council, moreover, imposed restrictions on the granting of indulgences, but Innocent conceded them to pilgrims to Rome and Compostela and to those providing ships for the crusaders.

The theory of indulgences, as developed shortly afterwards by the scholastics, was based on the idea of vicarious satisfaction. The Church appeared as the trustee of the treasury of merits already gained by Christ and the saints, making up for the expiation to which ordinary sinners were bound but which they could not or would not accomplish. It must always be emphasized that, in the theory of indulgences, it was never sin itself which was claimed to be forgiven, but the penalty resulting from sin. Forgiveness is also normally linked with some personal act by which the indulgence is inserted into the traditional scheme of "redemptions", that is, the possibility of partially transforming the penance due into works of another kind which are generally easier for the person concerned to perform.

At the beginning, indulgences as a rule were attached to extraordinary accomplishments: the Crusade, for example. But since the gaining of a privilege of this kind was in principle more burdensome than the original penance, the historical law of diminishing returns set in and it finally became sufficient to make small monetary gifts or to say a prayer. Nevertheless, it must be noted that it was not the fact of a monetary gift as such—not even the contribution to the building of St Peter's, which was the occasion of Luther's attack—which led to a distortion of the idea of indulgences. This came about much more as a result of the entanglement of the Western Church in the innumerable political and commercial affairs of "Christendom". The indulgence preached at Wittenberg, for example, was not intended as a means only of contributing to the building of St Peter's, but also of covering the debts incurred by the Archbishop of Mainz in order to become a cardinal. The application of indulgences, like the penalty of excommunication, could also be made to serve the Church's political aims. We know that, at the time of the Counter-Reformation, even confession—particularly if the penitent was a prince—was used in the interests of the wars of religion.

2. Pope Alexander II's indulgence for the Spanish warriors (1063) marks the date at which the Roman central government formally approved and took under its wing the religious war, born out of the Spanish struggle for existence against the Moors. In this way, Islam's militant religious spirit entered into Western Christianity as a whole. It is interesting to note that Gregory VII already organized in this form

also the internal struggle against the Church's enemies, against the imperial ecclesiastical policy, and first of all in the conflict of the *Pataria* with the Archbishop of Milan, who had been appointed by the Emperor.[15] By limiting the Holy War to the Crusade properly so-called, Urban II a generation later considerably modified the situation in a way that might have taken the sting out of the perpetual internal civil war between Pope and Emperor. In fact, this modification turned out to be temporary: the crusade was preached against both the Albigensians and the Hohenstaufens, thus being again magnified into a holy war and one fought indeed on Christian soil.

In the Crusade also a new warrior-*élite* found its Christian form: the Knights of the Cross. These had their roots as much in Christian monasticism as in the Moslem *almoravides*[16]—professional, celibate soldiers, who are mostly remembered in Europe in the final but distorted form of the Turkish janissaries. The union of monastery and barracks (*ribat*), which had already appeared in Moslem Spain, did not find there directly its Christian counterpart. For the three famous Spanish orders of chivalry—of Alcántara, Calatrava and Santiago—were formed as national groups (in this respect being comparable to the Teutonic Knights), inspired by the example of the international Templars and Knights of St John which had arisen in Palestine, succeeding these chronologically or at any rate immediately.

The reason for this development here seems to be that at the beginning of the Spanish resistance—almost four centuries earlier—a total mobilization against the Moors was alone sufficient to meet the difficult situation: a more limited expedition, as in the Palestinian crusades, would have failed. Faith in Santiago Matamoros aimed at this exaltation of the whole people and even at a later date we find a far larger number with the rank of knighthood and therefore a much poorer class of petty knights than in other European countries. The petty knight-class also lived largely on the memories of the religious wars, which still played an important part in the colonization of the New World: the hunt for gold and possessions, which were indeed real factors already in the *reconquista* and in the Crusades, ought not simply to be invoked as arguments against this. Even the mad knight, Don Quixote, is essentially merely a crusader who has become an anachronism. On this Spanish soil, thoroughly soaked with the reality of the Holy War, the Knighthood of the Cross could not assume that specific and clearly defined importance which it had in the rest of Europe, where the knights were for most of the time concerned with more immediate and earthy aims at home.

Just as Peter Damian influenced the Roman Church in its adoption of the Irish penitential practices, so Bernard of Clairvaux was influential in the adoption of the new Knighthood of the Cross. It was he who drew up the rule of the Knights Templars. Once again, one of the most outstanding and best-known ascetics and mystics came out in support, not of an inward renewal, but of a new "solution", namely, the direct appointment of a monastic Order to the task of fighting for the faith. This combination of aims, given temporary expression in the Crusade, thus affected all Western chivalry and endowed it with something of the character of an Order, which found its appropriate and fascinating symbol in the Knighthood of the Grail described in epic poetry.

The fact that Bernard, the promoter of the Second Crusade (1147-49), did not want to take on the leadership himself, already incidentally revealed the hybrid character of a direct association of soldier and monk, Nevertheless, and although the Crusade preached by Bernard also failed, this new form of the Knighthood of the Cross persisted; indeed, it showed itself capable of undertaking other secular tasks over and above that directly of fighting, as we see from the success of the Knights Templar in financial matters, of the Knights of

St John in hospital work and—last but not least—of the Teutonic Order in founding a state on the colonial territory of Eastern Germany. Even when the Crusades properly so-called faded out, the fighting spirit of the crusaders lived on in a form transferred to the battle-ground within the Church. Not a little of this spirit entered into the formation of the later religious orders: the mendicant orders just as much as the Society of Jesus were *also* and indeed essentially battle-troops of the Pope, giving effect to his aims in both ecclesiastical and secular politics. To a large extent they were responsible for planting the spirit of a perpetual struggle for the faith in Western Christendom and repeatedly reviving it at the decisive moments of history.

3. The Germanic-primitive form of external religiosity, which had found its typical expression in the cult of relics, had become with the sapping of early Christian traditions so much the basis of living Christianity that the reform of the Church in its inner aspect had to set in at this point. Through it the traditions of the liturgical *corpus Christi* in the form of the Latin Mass and the Latin Office, which had become unintelligible, were largely and the study of the Latin Bible (the Vulgate) and the Latin Fathers wholly reserved and committed to the clergy and monks. With the codification of Canon Law the Church herself lost her total, world-embracing extension and was conceived as essentially the particular sphere of clergy and monks: her association with the whole body of Christians was outwardly maintained by a clerical supremacy, inwardly by the new form of Eucharistic piety. In an earlier chapter, we explained at length how this had been prepared by the practice of the cult of relics, which found there as it were a Christian centre and peak. We need only add that this Eucharistic piety was spread in the latter half of the twelfth century (that is, after Bernard of Clairvaux) particularly in the new Cistercian Order (and is not the least important distinction of this from what had

hitherto been a single Benedictine Order); that it had its dogmatic basis and was associated with the clerical Church in the teaching of the Fourth Lateran Council on transubstantiation; and that finally in the thirteenth century the mendicant orders promoted it and secured its general acceptance in Western Christianity.

4. There is a final point of great historical importance which must be mentioned. The reform of the Church, both in reducing this to a clerical institution and in the universal propagation of Eucharistic piety, could not take place without an alliance with philosophy. Philosophy had in the first place to make a critical survey and an arrangement of ecclesiastical tradition, which was embodied in a variety of mutually conflicting canons and patristic quotations. Hence, instead of merely collecting and arranging the material chronologically, an attempt was made to impose on it a systematic control with the aid of conceptual distinctions and general headings. Here lies the origin of the new systematic philosophy of the schools. But, in concrete instances also, the basic concepts of the objectification of the Church had to be clarified : for example, the Real Presence in the Eucharist, transubstantiation, the priestly character, the objective efficacy of the sacraments (*ex opere operato*).

Aristotelian logic, which was just then beginning to gain its ascendancy in the West, was available to deal with these tasks. It had the advantage over the hitherto dominant Platonic-Stoic philosophy of being much more down to earth, not beginning with an explanation of the world as a whole, but providing a conceptual structure for the mastery of concrete facts. Nevertheless, this conceptual structure was to an even greater degree worked out in terms of art or *techne* (technomorphous)[17] and therefore in the end also prevented a solution of the real problem. This was not the way to achieve either an historical perspective in general or a philosophy or theology of history which would in particular elucidate the reform of the Church which had just taken place. Aquinas, for instance, sometimes recognized the possibility of a change in the *status ecclesiae* and used it as an argument;[18] but it never occurred to him to use it as a principle for marking out the stages of the Church's history in a way similar to the distinction made in the early tradition of the Church between the stages of salvation-history in the Old and New Testaments. His blindness to history went so far that the exciting contemporary teaching of Abbot Joachim of Flora about the end of the Christian era could not stir him at least to recognize explicitly as a problem the close of an epoch in Church history. Nor did he think it necessary to produce a theory of the university, which appeared just at that time as an historical *novum* for the Church and the world and directly provided the basis of his own existence and activities.[19]

For these reasons an important stage in the history of ideas did not then reach its complete historical fulfilment, although Aquinas helped Aristotelian specialized philosophy (psychology, ethics, politics) to prevail finally against considerable resistance. He did recognize in principle for all time the secular spheres of life in their "relative" autonomy and restored to them their status as wholly legitimate ways to the "last end" of Christian teaching. But in fact they were understood in the light of Aristotelian theory and that philosopher began to enjoy the same authority in secular affairs as the Church possessed in matters of salvation. The Church, too, had the right to decide on the extent of the "relative" autonomy to be conceded to the secular spheres. Hence she was faced with a serious situation when Western man's experience of life and the world no longer fitted in to the Aristotelian scheme and when the State, economic life and learning could no longer be affected by censures—such as had been launched, for example, against Philip IV of France and Galileo. It was only then that the scholastic authorization of a real autonomy of secular existence could be carried out—but precisely by departing from the authoritative scholastic conceptual scheme. The same autonomy could be maintained within those limits inherent in human reason, where the Church with her normative language handed down from the past had to be content with a cautious attempt to remain in the game and with a moral-theological evaluation of secular initiatives.

IX

The Protest of the *Ecclesia Spiritualis*

THE existing forms in which Christianity had found historical expression were brought together under the control of the Roman central government and thus made universal: the Western Church was therefore able to retain her leading place in Christendom, in spite of her simultaneous withdrawal from this in its wholeness into a more limited field, distinguished and set apart from the rest by the seven sacraments at the centre and the new Canon Law of the clerical society at the periphery. It was this more restricted sphere alone which could properly be regarded as the Church and no longer the whole living reality of Christendom. Thus, within the life of the Church understood in this sense, there came about an enormous systematization: from the functionalism of the priestly hierarchy, by way of the formalization of the sacraments, to the formal obedience of the simple faithful.

This de-personalizing of Christianity was further strengthened by the fact that even the secular sphere was not left open to free initiative. As "Christendom" and therefore as the scene of the Church's activity, it remained subject to her normative and moral influence, neither of which needed to be adapted to secular realities. The most powerful influence on personal life remained indeed the appeal to the *ratio peccati*; but, while it had a salutary effect in keeping down immorality, it was less effective in promoting and confirming personal initiative, always fraught with moral dangers—least of all when this initiative did not seem to fit in unconditionally with the traditional scheme laid down by the Church for action in the world.

Against this de-personalizing process there was heard within the Church the protest of the sectaries, providing in the second millennium of Church history the same sort of foil which the competition of Gnosticism presented in early Christianity. The sectaries firmly maintained that the personal factor, not the institutional, was decisive for the existence of a Church which had to confront the world as essentially a community of saints. From the Donatists in Constantine's time onwards they had tried to make the situation of persecuted Christianity the norm also for a world which at least claimed to have become Christian and in which they were persecuted now, not only by the State, but also by the Church. Thus they were forced into the position of questioning in the name of the "true" Church the Christian character of the Church which persecuted them. In so far as the Reformation refrained from demonstrating personal holiness through moral or ascetic behaviour, but on the other hand made it of primary importance in the form of a justice imputed through faith in Jesus Christ, it also gave a sharp impact to the personal protest; this, however, was balanced by the retention of important institutional elements. Thus among the reformed Churches also the personal element could be more powerfully directed outwardly into the world, while among the sects properly so-called it was largely exhausted in the process of building up the community.

In the Middle Ages the decisive controversy on the two possible ways of shaping Christianity took place within the Franciscan Order, which had arisen in the same intellectual climate as the Waldensians and, moreover, for nearly a century immediately after the death of St Francis felt strongly attracted by the fascination of sectarianism. For the famous controversy between the two parties in the Order—the Spirituals and the Conventuals—was no mere harmless and petty monkish squabble without interest today, but a continuation of the discussion of our theme: namely, whether

Christianity had to be predominantly personal or institutional.[1] But what really occasioned the controversy was the fact that St Francis on the one hand placed his new community as an Order under the Pope and, on the other, forbade in his will any alteration to the rule he had himself laid down. The rule required a complete abandonment of possessions, not on the part only of the individual Franciscan, but also of the Order as a whole. But the latter requirement simply cannot be realized in the present state of the world: here we reach a point at which monasticism itself is shown to be tied to this world and therefore cannot fulfil the mission of representing the eschatological end-situation. Hence, it was only a few years after the death of St Francis that Pope Gregory IX, who had been his patron, decided in favour of the institutional interpretation—which had to be considered as essential both for the Church and for her Orders. Even the rule of an Order and the testament of a saint, declared the Pope, did not have the same binding force as the Gospel, but merely emphasized selected points: the prohibition of ownership, as far as the Order was concerned, could be considered satisfied by the use of a credit system and by appointing a layman as agent in the transactions.

As a result of this papal decision, a cleavage arose in the Order and the "Spirituals"—who held strictly to the saint's will—were brought more and more into conflict with the Pope and with the Church as a whole. After decades of bitter controversy, Pope John XXII in 1323 declared heretical the assertion that Christ and his disciples had possessed nothing either privately or in common. This recognition of ownership on the part of the medieval Church corresponds to her recognition of matrimony against the early Gnostics and their descendants in the Middle Ages, the Albigensians.

The controversy about ownership and the institutional character of Church and Orders became so important in principle mainly because it was bound up with a still deeper question which came to a head in the tense eschatological expectation of the thirteenth century. This had been crystallized in the prophetic teaching of the Calabrian Abbot Joachim of Flora: he claimed that in the year 1260, after the theological age of the Old and New Testaments, a "third kingdom" of the Holy Spirit would follow in which for the first time the pure meaning of the Gospel would be understood and given full effect by a new monastic order. This "third kingdom" or "reign" of the Holy Spirit, after the past kingdoms of the Father and the Son, became the prototype of all the world-historical Utopias of the Enlightenment and of the nineteenth century;[2] even Hitler's "Third Reich" owes something to this tradition, as also does the more important though less well-known belief in its fulfilment in the age of technical perfection. But this is not what interests us here.

Joachim had prophesied as a necessary prelude and introductory event to his "third kingdom" the foundation of a new Order of the Spirit by an extraordinary saint, whose authority for the coming third age would be equal to that of Moses for the Old Testament and of Jesus Christ for the New (the age presumably coming to an end in 1260). When such an extraordinary saint had come to the fore in the person of Francis of Assisi—who, in fact, could be seen to be "Christlike" through his unique privilege of the stigmata—nothing was easier than to see the prophecy as fulfilled in him. As a result of linking up the saint and his Order in this way with the idea of the "third kingdom", the controversy on ownership became much more acute and even dangerous to the very existence of the Church. The Spirituals were inclined to venerate in Francis actually a new Christ, whose authority now exceeded that of Christ or his Vicar, the Pope. The rule and the will of their founder were claimed as the constitutional documents of the "third kingdom", by which the eschatological consummation was made evident already in the sphere of earthly history.

Finally, the controversy between Spirituals and Conventuals was treated as one on the different theories of the historical *locus* of the Church and her saints. All agreed that the Christian status of the world as represented by the Church was not final. But while the Church in her sacramental nature considered herself for all time to come as the authoritative defender of a revelation completed in Christ, her "spiritual" opponents believed that a new, but certainly final revelation of the Holy Spirit was to be given by the saint who would inaugurate the "third kingdom". According to this theory the perfection of the final state, the ultimate ground of all Christian hope, would not be attained only *eschatologically* through catastrophe and the end of the present world, but through the saint and his Order had already begun *historically* in this world. History in its present working out had already to possess eschatological finality in itself, not merely in the perspective of a hidden, transcendent end and goal. The peril and charm of this claim lay not least in the fact that it still echoed something of the barely vanished tradition of the imperial Church : in the legacy the fiction was maintained of the possibility of a thorough and total christianization of the existing world in another form, less burdened by earthly obstacles. The secular-ecclesiastical unity of the imperial Church was really the form which was to be superseded by the new revelation. For the rest of time, the new Order of the Spirit would then be the historical-social as well as the eschatological and ultimate form of salvation-history.

Anyone who casts the weight of his sympathy too readily on the side of the Spirituals ought to be quite clear as to what their victory would have meant for the world. Reflection of this kind of course presupposes that the victory was in fact possible at all : a very dubious presumption since it would have struck not only at the Church's "power-politics", but also at all conceivable secular interests. On its own principles, it would have meant if not the actual end of the world, then at least the ideological. From this time onwards nothing "worldly" would have arisen to confront the "spiritual", and nothing "spiritual" would have been able any longer to find its expression in the field of secular culture. Dante (1265-1325) and Giotto (1276-1337), on whose shoulders (in spite of Dante's secret sympathy for the Spirituals) Humanism and the Renaissance rest, would then have been impossible or at least have been without any historical importance: Dante and Giotto, who as laymen precisely in these decisive years, forsaking the aureate Byzantine style, set out to symbolize the mystery of Christianity in a new and notably secular language. Albert the Great and Aquinas likewise would scarcely have succeeded in making Aristotelianism prevail against Plato and Augustine: in other words, the justification in principle of secular activity as "edifying" for the Christian and for Christianity would not have been assured. The development of new, autonomous sciences—especially the basic natural and historical sciences—was indeed held up, but not completely blocked by the Church, and in the course of time the opposition was worn down; but the victory of the Spirituals would have meant, as in Islam, turning attempts at scientific progress into heresy and thus bringing about their complete failure. There is no need to pursue this point further: it is evident that the acceptance of the intellectual claim of the Spirituals was impossible from both the human and the ecclesiastical standpoints.

Nevertheless, in this respect also, the Church paid a high, a very high price for rejecting an attempt at a solution which had its own attraction and was deeply rooted in the Christian tradition itself. Joachim of Flora and the Spirituals had appealed against the historical situation of the Church, albeit in an unacceptable fashion, to two truths of the Christian faith: eschatology and the Holy Spirit. Both truths thus became suspect, not only because they had been so directly linked with history and associated with the claims of the Spirituals, but as dangerous in themselves. From this time onwards, both eschatological expectation and awareness of the presence of the Holy Spirit, which had never been among the most carefully cultivated Christian beliefs, except for some fragmentary remains, now practically disappeared out of the life of the Christian.

At the height of the Middle Ages, eschatology provided at least the background for the Christian Empire, as this was still represented in the Hohenstaufen period by the *Ludus de Antichristo*. People knew the generally accepted interpretation of 2 Thessalonians 2.6-7, according to which the Roman Empire alone held back Antichrist and, as soon as the last Emperor had laid down his crown at the holy sepulchre in Jerusalem, he would descend on the world. Now that both the Holy Roman Empire and the *ecclesia spiritualis* had been brought down, no one thought any longer of Antichrist, but only of death and the fate of the individual in the next world.[3] The fact that Luther was then bold enough to see again the coming of Antichrist—and in fact, in the person of the Pope—made the idea completely intolerable for the Roman Church. She did indeed insist all the more on her assurance of the presence of the Holy Spirit, but this official support more or less exhausted his function. His living presence in the soul of the Christian was certainly taught and even emphasized in the form of a sacrament, but this presence seemed completely secondary to that by which he gave an official guarantee to papal and conciliar definitions. For the spiritual life of the Christian the presence of the Holy Spirit was overshadowed by the "Real Presence" in the Eucharist and had little or no power to rouse his initiative. By contrast with Christmas and Easter, Pentecost remained an unintelligible feast from which it was scarcely possible to derive a Christian meaning.

All this meant, however, that the Church was in danger of losing the whole background of her existence. Against Joachim and the Spirituals she had rightly asserted herself as the authentic institution of salvation until the second coming of Christ, but this coming seemed again to have been postponed to the completely unforeseeable future; it had scarcely any effect now on earthly time. The future appearance of Christ, like the presence of the Holy Spirit, was almost completely thrust out of the minds of the people by the Eucharistic Presence. The rejection of the claim to finality on the part of Joachim and the Spirituals seemed to mean the assertion of the same claim on the part of the Church on earth, concealing the essential transitoriness of her existence, which had to cease with the second coming of Christ. But in this way the earthly dimensions of the Church (visible, historical, Roman, etc.) became largely isolated from her transcendent background and gained in themselves a preponderance which easily led to a positivistic interpretation of her nature and brought her permanently to the verge of a "sociological misunderstanding". The distinction between her "sacramental nature" and the historical attitudes which she took up in the sphere of politics and philosophy became in practice impossible to establish; equally impossible were realistic discussion and the justification of these attitudes from the appropriate historical standpoints. The states of the Church and scholastic philosophy, for instance, became almost matters of faith. The Church largely lost her transcendental permeability and gained instead a massive self-sufficiency, being content to draw up statistics of membership and the reception of the sacraments and scarcely considering it necessary to restrict herself and her action to symbolizing what was mediated through her—although this is precisely what ought to have resulted from the institutionalization brought about by the ecclesiastical reforms.

As a result of the divisions created by the Reformation and

the wars of religion which followed it, the sociological misunderstanding of the Church was increased in every way. The situation seemed to demand an unconditional assertion and upholding of the most unreal claims. Thus the Church presented an abundance of easy targets to the total attack of the Enlightenment. But even this storm passed over, because it was impossible to give credibility to the new rationalist myths and thus replace the rejected dogmas. Hence, after the disappointments of the French Revolution, Europe was held back in every field in a state of pure positivism which then provided itself with a myth in the shape of a belief in progress, not indeed very profound, but for that very reason so much the more accessible. Basically this nineteenth century positivism was merely taking stock of the remnants left behind after the disappearance of the transcendent background.

The Churches struggled fiercely against this positivism, but without lasting success. They scarcely noticed that their comparative powerlessness was due to the fact that they had for a long time justified their own existence mainly from the same standpoint and therefore had to share the responsibility for the positivist deviation of the nineteenth century.[4] Of course, their situation could have been saved, since they might at any time have appealed to their "proper" or transcendent nature. But when an attempt was made to do this already in the nineteenth century, it was another picture which dominated the foreground. The Roman Church especially, defending herself against her persecutors, held doggedly to all the positions which had been attacked and continued to foster the sociological misunderstanding.

X

The New Historical Situation

The Transmuting of Western Christianity

THE stage of development which Christianity had reached already in the thirteenth century involved an inner contradiction. On the one hand, it had succeeded in splitting up the political and cultural unity which had taken shape and on the whole been maintained under the rule of a sacred kingship. Moreover, the process had gone so far that not only was public life divided off into the two spheres of Church and State, but there was also a rift at the very heart of personal and social life: the Christian was bound simultaneously by two loyalties, matrimony, for instance, in regard to its spiritual substance and its "civil effects" being placed under two diverse jurisdictions. And yet, on the other hand, Western civilization was maintained as an historical unity and indeed as a Christian historical unity. First of all, through the ambiguity of a spiritual-secular Church, which not only claimed to be the protector of tradition, the sacraments and morality, but also attempted as the "supreme" social unity to assert its power to judge political and cultural matters; then through the spontaneous recognition of this dual primacy of the Church in "Christendom", even on the part of the late medieval cities—largely economically and politically independent—and of modern states.

Even for the first two centuries after the Reformation, in spite of the theoretical opposition between the divided Churches, there was no fundamental change in the actual situation but only a territorial-confessional cleavage within Christendom[1]: a fact which, in the last resort, may be explained by the original intention of the Reformers to reform the Church as a whole and not to set up particular Churches alongside the Roman. It was only when the establishment of the reformed Church as a single whole was seen to be impracticable that the territorial division of three confessions arose; the Church of England could be regarded as a fourth, but represented on the whole a final and absolutist form of the early medieval regional Church. In each of the confessional regions the ecclesiastical-social "unity of Christendom" was for a long time maintained as the norm or—when struggling against the supremacy of another confession—was at least sought after.

It was only the "Enlightenment", emerging out of the continuous internal and external political civil war of the confessional states, which succeeded after the "Glorious Revolution" of 1688 in restricting the State religion in such a way as to set an example for later times and in making more or less serious inroads on the dogmatic and ritual traditions of Christianity. And it was not until the nineteenth century that the Industrial Revolution undermined, along with the basic factors of life as hitherto known, also the thousand-year-old "Christian morality" of the West. We need not follow all the variations of pace and development in this process, but we may point out that the attempt also of Catholicism to escape its consequences by mobilizing its members for a restoration of the old system in the long run did not succeed and in fact never could have succeeded.

It was by an attack from outside that the Enlightenment and the Industrial Revolution undermined more and more the traditions of Christian Europe. Within the unity of the system of "Christendom" both had been, as we might say, forgotten or—better—not foreseen. The Enlightenment in its scholastic form was indeed built into the system, but its logical consequence—"free thought"—had been rejected (as

131

we know, Calvin was no less hostile than the Pope himself to such trends). It had obtained its historical opportunity simply through the long-drawn-out and indecisive confessional civil war. There came a stage at which the confessions were resigned to one another's existence and what had hitherto been the dead angle between their fronts—human reason—was able to become the soil of unforeseen hope for a better world. This sudden outbreak of historical optimism then also united the Enlightenment with the Industrial Revolution, which not only promised a better world, but was charming it little by little into existence. This new world did not even emerge out of the neglected issues of confessional strife, but arose quite on the side, on what we may call virgin territory, which in fact also gained its epoch-making importance mainly by providing a way out of the now barren controversies.

Historically speaking, the confessional struggle had ceased to be important. The Enlightenment and the Industrial Revolution were able to seize the opportunity to break into the world of Western Christianity and even to exploit the situation to build up a "new world". But this revolutionary impact is only a part of their influence on the West. They were in no sense *merely* an expedient or a new hope and still less a deceptive illusion. Behind them lay a force of conviction which they drew out of the tradition of Western Christianity itself. They, too, may be regarded as the consequence of Western Christianity—indeed, from one aspect, as its essential and historically unique consequence.[2] It was not entirely without reason that the Enlightenment claimed to be real or practical Christianity and in the eighteenth century became so mingled with this as to be scarcely distinguishable from it. It was only from the consequences of the Enlightenment—namely, from the experience of the French Revolution—that it could be recognized as something essentially different from the Christianity of German Idealism and Romanticism. This diagnosis in turn, as it took on a restorative form, was inclined to overlook the Christian background of the Enlightenment.

Western Christianity provided a negative rather than a positive justification for the Enlightenment and the Industrial Revolution: it was they who "transmuted" it, who caused it to "emerge". After it had struggled—*also*, but still very thoroughly—at enormous moral, social and political expense, to make man and his world endurable, the Enlightenment suddenly and with great pathos presented it with the claim that the natural man (Rousseau), and even the Jew (Lessing) and the savage (Seume), were better men: in other words, that the thousand-year-old exertions of Western Christianity had brought about a merely negative result. The Industrial Revolution then provided direct evidence—becoming more convincing the longer it was studied—that what was considered to be the normal state of the world under the domination of Christianity was scarcely on a higher level than that of late antiquity: in view of the progress then beginning, it had to be described as "underdeveloped", and a "better world" without the interference of the restrictive influences of Christian faith and morals was to be established solely by the application of technical understanding and a clearly defined discipline of work.

It was particularly impressive that the childhood ailments of the industrial world, which still led even in the nineteenth century to essentially temporary difficulties and to gloomy and revolutionary utterances, were more and more eliminated by technical progress itself. Thus there was spread the idea of an effortless existence in a world which could be manipulated at will, an idea which was very credible and which had all the greater seductive power in as much as no decisive counterpart could be offered from the Christian side. For, according to the prevailing Christian morality, there could be no objection to the use of technical things if only because this was expressly a question of *adiaphora* (that is, morally indifferent objects); and, in this world of inconceivable abundance, the traditional impulse to asceticism also lost that natural credibility which it had in a world largely sterile and needy. Finally, the basic theological notion of salvation was confronted with a world which no longer appeared primarily to be in need of it, but claimed to be "perfect" or at least on the way to a kind of perfection: a world in which death still appeared as a painful event, but also as an incidental risk which might be indefinitely postponed, in the meantime applying every effort to get rid of the remaining wants and discomforts by the constant improvement of technical aids.

It is not too difficult, in the last resort, to lay bare the illusory character of this amalgamation of "enlightened" reason with technical progress, supported by a Christian conception of a final consummation; but it must be admitted that this is not possible simply in the name of Western Christianity, but only in the light of historical reason—which is not yet effective on a wide scale—or of bitter experience. Western Christianity as such is not capable of intervening in this process nor is it justified in doing so; for, in virtue of its still insufficiently clarified sociological misunderstanding, it was itself present at the birth.

Since Augustine's time and particularly after Charlemagne's oversimplified interpretation of his thought, Western Christianity has been convinced of the possibility of promoting the kingdom of God on earth by direct means. Not only the Christian Empire, but also the papal theocracy, Lutheranism, revolutionary Calvinism and finally the "political Catholicism" of the nineteenth century,[3] lived on the strength of this conviction, if not as a dogmatic belief, then at least as an historical assumption. Now that Christianity since the eighteenth century has been confronted with the secularized final hopes of the Enlightenment and the technical world, it can prove its historical right to be consulted in the future only by revoking the short-sightedness of the past. It can show its secularized descendants that, in spite of all progress and all that has been accomplished, there can still be no talk of a kingdom of God on earth; but it must itself recognize that the kingdom simply is not to be realized on earth at all. That is to say: Christianity must not only preach to its earthly, historical partners the recognition of the transitoriness of all earthly things but must itself accept this state of affairs. This holds not only for its activity in the outer world, but also for its ecclesiastical organization and even for its "sacramental nature". For although the sacraments may outlast the varied succession of historical epochs and of the historically changing *status ecclesiae* as "the same Church" (*eadem ecclesia*),[4] they still do not outlast the historical *status* of the world as such, since, according to the teaching of the Church, they give way in the kingdom of God to *that* to which—without prejudice to their present divine power—they point here below. This regained consciousness of the sacraments as pointing beyond themselves together with the renewed awareness of the ultimate powerlessness of Christianity in the earthly-social sphere, as the revelation of Antichrist in the Apocalypse presents it to faith, may be the characteristic of a future, credible Christianity distinguishing it from what we have hitherto known as the Christianity of the West.

In view of our recent experience of totalitarianism, which has brought the reality of Antichrist out of the impenetrability of an article of faith into the visibility of a possible political action, such an honourable if not wholly pleasant admission may be impossible to avoid. In this respect, it is particularly worthy of note that totalitarian states in usurping ecclesiastical functions (as the Fascist theory of the State more or less openly asserted, by claiming the character of *ecclesiasticità*),[5] among other things, permitted the revival of practices which they had learned from the Christian State or from the Church at the time of their historical power. It has often been observed that Mussolini, Hitler and Goebbels came from Catholic backgrounds and that Stalin had been a student for the priesthood. The ambivalence of power, as well as of every faith historically established, has thus become clear through such experiences for anyone who can and will see. But it is also clear that, no matter how powerfully equipped Christianity or the Church may be, it must in the end be the loser in competition with the consistent practice of a totalitarian State. Although there is much that can be questioned in the past history of Western Christianity, its presuppositions made one thing impossible: it could not, like the totalitarian State, indulge as a matter of course in the persistent practice of lying and violence.

The Sacredness of Personality

In a work on the history of Western Christianity, we cannot fail to call attention to the new world-situation which has arisen precisely through its historical results and which in turn presents quite new problems for Christianity itself. The world has become a conglomeration of autonomous, objective and impersonal-functional associations, with the running of which the moral responsibility of the individual human being can be charged only to a very limited degree. Certainly there is an urgent need of bringing the network of these functional associations within the law in such a way that their smooth running is assured without at any rate destroying the reality and the possibility of a sphere of personal life. But this is a task which also calls just as much for an understanding of reality and a capacity for spiritual perception and initiative as for moral judgment; and it can in fact be accomplished only by the co-operation of small circles of people equipped and authorized to undertake it. And yet, even if it were accomplished—which is scarcely the case at present—a technical world made endurable would

still be a completely profane world, by its very nature beyond the global control of morality and still more of the
higher demands of a sacral order.

In this secularized world, the human person is placed in
a situation dangerous in practice, but ontologically privileged. His supreme moral obligation can only be to recognize
and maintain his privileged status in a heterogeneous world.
At a time when the traditional forces of habit and custom
have largely disappeared with the loss of organic ties, the
supreme importance also for morality of man's special equip-
ment—his reason—has come to be recognized. It seems that
today there is no longer a self-evident morality secured by
social relationships to protect man's status, but only that
which results from a comparatively high degree of awareness and discernment. The primacy of the spirit over politics
could become therefore a characteristic of the new age of
the world.

In addition, the Christian is promised as a special endowment the aid of the Holy Spirit. From the very beginning he
is placed in the world as a sacred person. At this point we may
perhaps recall the fact that the theological doctrine of the
procession of the Holy Spirit is one of the very few dogmatic
differences between the Eastern and the Western Church.
And even this point of difference, although raised already by
Photius, played no part in the schism of 1054 and became
acute only at the time of the Crusades.[6] However this difference may be interpreted theologically with reference to
the internal relations of the three divine Persons, in the West
the formula of the *filioque* (as distinct from the Eastern *per
filium*) seems to involve a claim to world-mastery and an
early awareness—in spite of the distinction between the
spiritual and the secular—of the religious importance for the
Christian also of the profane world. For by naming Father
and Son as co-equal principles of the Holy Spirit the direct
line from the world as event to the salvation-event is ex-

cluded: there is reserved to the Father as Creator a permanent religious importance which is not included in the redemptive act of the Son. Looked at in this way, the *filioque* seems to imply the fact (the ontological aspect of which has been mentioned above) that man's relationship to God is at once sacramental and more than sacramental.

Nevertheless, this immediate relationship also to God, which, according to Christian teaching, is realized precisely in a profane world as something regained through the redemption, is sacramentally anchored in the Church. From this point of view, two sacraments which have led a notoriously apocryphal existence in Western Christianity—Confirmation and Matrimony—now acquire a new importance. In the reformed Churches both had completely ceased to be regarded as sacraments. In the Roman Church they were in fact administered and received, even given a particularly striking setting: in the first, in what remained for the simple Christian generally a unique confrontation, the bishop administered the sacrament; in the second, the parties themselves conferred it in what was an equally unique exercise of ecclesiastical office.[7] Yet both sacraments remained almost completely hidden behind those which held a foremost place in the Church and were rendered more prominent by their repetition, namely, Penance and the sacrament "of the Altar"; they were less obvious also because the emphasis lay not on their administration and reception, but on the status which they conferred and their assurance of strength precisely in the midst of life in the world. The fact that, once received, without the mediation of any further ecclesiastical functions, they set up a permanent and direct relationship precisely of secular life to the world beyond this, was brought out only very inadequately in an epoch when the Church was largely identified with the clergy.

The effect attributed to Confirmation, of making the Christian into a "soldier of Christ", dramatizes the event in the light of the picture of the *militia Christi* which came into fashion in the time of persecution. It ought not to be interpreted—or at any rate only in exceptional circumstances—as a challenge to fight for the Church's internal interests, as "political Catholicism" was inclined to do. The effects of the Holy Spirit within the Church—for example, in the infallible teaching office or in Ordination to the priesthood—are special gifts, according to the Church's teaching, and are not ascribed to the sacrament of Confirmation. This is seen primarily as the source of the seven gifts of the Spirit, six of which are enumerated for the first time in Isaiah 11.2. It is significant that not less than four of these gifts (wisdom, knowledge, understanding and counsel) belong to man's rational nature, to his cognitive activity in regard to the world and the situation in which he is placed. Fortitude and the fear of the Lord are also clearly related to the world and therefore we may presume that the gift of piety —which has been added to the prophet's list—receives its special nuance precisely from the secular application of the rest of the gifts. By the exercise of the gifts the Church is not constituted in the first place, but given reality in the life of the world: to the extent that the gifts are effective in this way, Confirmation gives the layman the right to be consulted in the Church. "The formation of the *civitas terrena*" cannot be regarded as an adequate description of the layman's task; apart from the fact that it is altogether too general in an epoch of cultural oases, the formula undermines the essentially Christian witness and realization which can emerge in virtue of the sacrament of Confirmation.[8]

The meaning of Matrimony, the second sacrament directed to life in the world, has also not been fully appreciated in Western Christianity—for a variety of reasons. One of these is that marriage is a legacy from a pre-Christian world: when compared with monastic and priestly celibacy, it was explained not in the light of its essential goodness so much as something less perfect; preaching has been less concerned with the immense scope offered by its qualities of unity and indissolubility than with their role as moral barriers against infidelity and divorce. Today the omnipresent network of technical automatisms has placed an almost intolerable strain on the conduct of human life and has thus thrown new light on the exceptionally personal character and—viewed objectively—the quite improbable heroism of every venture into marriage. In any case the emphasis in married life from the Christian standpoint has shifted from the moral factor, which hitherto alone counted, to the more basic physical and social factors: it is here, too, that the main reasons for the modern crisis of marriage may be sought.

In the present work, all we can do is to call attention to this state of affairs. But in an epoch which urges those who have the vocation for it to apply their mind to the mastery of its difficulties, we cannot neglect the special obligation of pointing out that marriage with someone who lacks this vocation is almost certain to lead to a *capitis diminutio*: the association forbidden as a misalliance in the class-society of the past may now have become in a different form and situation a new and very serious problem which is also of absolutely fundamental importance to morality. In this respect, it must again be recalled that Matrimony of its nature excludes other sexual relationships, but not human contacts altogether, and that it can maintain its sacramental character precisely by mastering also that danger of insular exclusiveness to which existence in cultural oases is particularly exposed. The almost religious isolation of the family, as in the Protestant tradition, can scarcely be the best way of facing the most varied forms of technical allurement—including well-meant educational and ecclesiastical schemes organized by the factory.

In closing, we must note with surprise the fact that adoption plays an embarrassing role in Western Christianity, occurring in families without natural offspring, and not—as in pre-Christian Rome—a constructive role in society. This is all the more astonishing in view of the teaching of Christian theology that man's basic quality through grace is that of being an adopted child.

The Justification of the Modern World

The historical results of the Enlightenment and the Industrial Revolution obviously surpass those of the thousand-year-old political and moral exertions of Western Christianity. It is in this fact that their attraction lies, not least also for the broad masses. For it was precisely the broad and solid basis of what had hitherto been a Christian society—the ordinary people, in whom in nineteenth-century Germany, for instance, both Bismarck and Bishop Ketteler* still placed their hopes—it was this people which had now been violently deprived of its traditions.

The essential problems become visible indeed only at a level above this "social question" and therefore generally remain concealed from the "man in the street" and from a Christianity involved in a sociological misunderstanding. For at this higher level of both philosophy and historical science it becomes clear that there is not only a dubious power of attraction proper to the Enlightenment and the Industrial Revolution, but also an indisputable historical right. Although they broke into the thought and social structure of Western Christianity from outside, they are both equally legitimate historical results precisely of that Christi-

---

* Wilhelm Emmanuel Ketteler (1811–77) was consecrated Bishop of Mainz in 1850. He devoted the bulk of his efforts to freeing the Church in Germany from control by the State and played a prominent role in the *Kulturkampf*. He also had a keen concern for social questions, and in 1864 published a book discussing the problem of the Church and the proletariat (*Die Arbeiterfrage und das Christentum*). At the First Vatican Council he opposed the promulgation of the dogma of papal infallibility as inopportune and returned to Germany before the vote was taken. Subsequently, however, he accepted the dogma.

anity. This, as we have already explained, destroyed on the one hand the unity of existence embodied in the Empire by making a decisive separation between the "spiritual" and the "secular" and on the other struggled to maintain "Christendom" as a secular unity of existence under ecclesiastical rule.

Against this ambiguity of a schizophrenic unity there arose from the time of the Middle Ages—partly as incidental by-products, but nevertheless quite logically—the new claims of a thoroughly secular world and of a secularized intellect, both of which had to take their stand outside the social unity of Christendom. This trend appeared first of all in the form of heterodox teaching (as in Berengarius' doctrine of the Eucharist) and sectarian schisms (as with the Franciscan Spirituals). It led in the theories (but not at first in practice) of the Reformation Churches to a radical opposition between "the spirit" and "the world". This tendency shaped decisively the course of history, but the development was far from being dramatic or notably "Protestant", taking the form of a scarcely noticed colonization at the edge of the Christian world.

Here newly discovered virgin soil was won and worked up with stubborn efforts for the spiritual and secular claims emerging outside the wholeness of Christendom, but nevertheless derived from it. This radical transformation, completely changing the basis of historical existence, was possible only against the background of Western Christianity; and, within the scope of world history as a whole, it did in fact occur only on European soil or on soil colonized by Europeans. Here in the last resort is the reason for Europe's historical intellectual primacy, a primacy which cannot be destroyed either by philosophical theories of universal humanity or by internecine strife in the West. The Enlightenment and the Industrial Revolution mark the point of time at which this hitherto clandestine settlement at the periphery of Christendom became evident and led in its results to a new historical epoch. Formally, this epoch can be distinguished from earlier Western Christianity as post-Christian, from earlier Europe as post-European and from earlier history as post-historical. The Janus-headed character of this new epoch, not apparent either to the undialectical "man in the street" or to the unhistorical "intellectual", consists in the fact—which we merely mention here—that it is also predetermined in its antecedents as Christian, European and historical.

Max Weber's pioneer work has made it clear that the Industrial Revolution was conditional on what he called the "disenchantment of the world": that is, through Christianity, the world (apart from the quantitatively limited field of the sacraments) was deprived in principle of its sacred character and delivered up in its profane reality to man as ontologically superior. This in fact occurred only within Western Christianity and therefore it was only from here also that man's technical dominion over the world could be established. The possibility of cutting off this "seizure of power" from its historical antecedents and transferring it into an atmosphere of quite different beliefs arises only at a later stage. But when such a transference does take place, cultural presuppositions of another kind—either the pagan assumption of a sacramental world or the Islamic conception of a world ruled by a Holy Law—are radically undermined by technical progress; even the dualism of the Eastern Church, with a sacred Christian sphere side by side with a world which is fundamentally evil and still unredeemed, becomes questionable—at least in Russia. Moreover, it becomes evident everywhere—even in the West, where the technical world began—that "man's dominion over nature" cannot be rendered absolute and be made into the basic phenomenon of existence, regardless of the range of human life as a whole, without very serious dangers arising for that very existence.

It is in fact humanity itself which is thus imperilled. Human existence was submerged in the first onrush of the "secondary system", which eluded the grasp of the hitherto dominant human and Christian morality and thus indirectly affected a higher level both of spirituality and of collective responsibility. To explain the problem in a brief formula, we might say: man's dominion over nature is in no way immoral, that is, it does not infringe the Ten Commandments and it can even be justified by the original command at Creation as related in Genesis. But that is no reason for regarding it as purely arbitrary, as an absolute and unconditional power of disposal over things. Morally, a higher discretion must intervene: as Paul expresses it in a lapidary sentence, "All things are lawful to me, but not all things are expedient" (1 Cor. 6.12, συμφέρει="contributes"). From the point of view of pastoral welfare, we can only say that Western Christianity has neglected precisely this problem of expediency in the comparatively simple field of organic relationships in the world and concentrated on very dubious religious routes: it will therefore be extraordinarily difficult to develop a higher discretion in the technical world, which presents itself to man with both a legitimate cosmic superiority of power and the illusion—difficult to penetrate—of being at his free disposal.

The decisive viewpoint of "expediency" refers precisely the human aspect of the problem back, so to speak, to the Enlightenment. Today it is mostly concealed by our concern for education and the right use of leisure, which have indeed a certain importance, but are secondary because they tend to shift the problem into the field of planned activity. It must be made clear again that the decisive field, which was sighted already in the time of the Enlightenment, is that of human liberty and spontaneity; but it is a sphere of both autonomy and responsibility and cannot reduce its tension or its challenge to the either-or of autonomy and heteronomy, as the philosophy of the Enlightenment supposed. Nevertheless, the truly Christian right of the Enlightenment to seize on "freedom" and "reason" must be emphasized.

That right is based on the fact that, in the Christian view, man and man *alone* out of all creatures, being superior to the whole inorganic, organic and naturally also technical world, is responsible for himself and this whole world submitted to his control. Moreover, Christian teaching also asserts that he is directly endowed with the character of eternity: this does not make him into the absolutely supreme being, as an unqualified humanism maintains, but does make him the supreme being in the visible world and places him in an immediate—and, in the Christian view, realizable— relationship with the one supreme Being. In spite of man's religious deficiencies, this character of eternity is superior to that which attaches to the sacraments: for these are relevant only to our time on this earth. This, incidentally, is the ontological explanation of the fact that man's relationship to God must be both sacramental and more than sacramental; and that the sacraments themselves are exposed to the danger of declining into a technomorphous organization if this "more" fails to come into operation or is even suppressed. It was the unquestionable right of the Enlightenment to stand for man's exceptional position in relation both to the world and even to the Church and to God: this right tends to turn into a threat only when man's mediate and immediate commitment is ignored.

The Threat to the Person

Although little has been heard of the dangers of technology, those created by the Enlightenment have been abundantly described from the time of the Romantic reaction. It must however be admitted that this occurred only *post factum*, namely, after the French Revolution had demonstrated to everyone the consequences of absolute freedom:

notably that which, following Hegel and after our experience of the totalitarian state, we call "terror". Until the French Revolution the people of the eighteenth century were also almost completely blind to the ambiguous nature of liberty, as we since the nineteenth century have been deceived by the ambiguity of the technical world.

The ambiguities of the Enlightenment lay in the fact that liberty and reason, after first being recognized precisely because of their transcendent reference as forces superior to the existing social world, lost this character of transcendent tension and appeared to be absolute and arbitrary human rights. The sociological misunderstanding of Christianity provided an obvious but short-sighted justification for abstracting from a sociologically compromising transcendence. In this form of secularized liberty and reason, the Enlightenment was brought by the American constitution and the French Revolution into a political and social system which was propagated as of universal human validity and, after its victory, became the foundation of the League of Nations and of the United Nations Organization. But the very specific roots of this system, which lay in the traditions of Western and especially Anglo-Saxon Christianity, were mostly revealed only after it had been adopted. Already on the continent of Europe the adoption of the system had produced critical situations, but its effect was more serious in the countries where the traditions of Western Christianity had no hold; for a freedom implicitly anchored in the conditions of a Christian society, when it entered an alien atmosphere, was very easily exposed to complete incomprehension or to a libertarian misinterpretation.

Our concern here is not the criticism of a system of secularized freedom and reason or even of its opponent, the totalitarian State. That is not to say that the question of a social system is a matter of indifference. But resistance, however well justified, to the danger of the totalitarian State is not primarily for the sake of another *system*, but to show that the latter offers considerably greater scope for the exercise of freedom. Freedom, however, in its true sense is not exercised at all within a system, but within a group of persons: for freedom is particularly the prerogative of persons. That also means: it begins mostly in a limited circle, in a small field, and it extends to society as a sum of personal achievements rather than as the product of any system claiming to be perfect. If there is to be a successful resistance to the danger of the totalitarian State itself, everything depends on whether it arises from the knowledge that no system—even a free system, even the ecclesiastical system—can itself secure freedom: it must be based on the realization that freedom is safeguarded only by persons and that they act in the light of possibilities which are always limited at any particular time. Liberty—particularly that which has a transcendent justification—is exposed in its social extension to the same danger of sociological misunderstanding as that which faces Christianity. Both are inevitably committed to a visible, social embodiment, but they cannot anticipate this —so to speak—*ante factum* in an already existing and complete social system. Just as no Christendom, however organized, can itself establish the fact of its Christianity, so no constitutional social system as such can prove the fact that freedom exists.

If, then, the future of Christianity like the future of liberty is dependent as much on persons as on institutions, it has to be recognized that neither can be fully realized. We have to be content here with a partial success, a realization that is limited to "islands", that is, to particular situations and within certain groups. Already, in the pre-technical world, all culture was distributed so to speak in oases in the naturally inhospitable primitive forest, steppe or desert. Every civilization tends to forget this fact and to consider itself as the norm of human existence. We have been misled especially by the conception of the ancient and the Christian oases as "universal" into thinking that this universality is biologically and statistically an attribute of human existence as such. The fact that culture has hitherto been distributed in oases has been brought home to us only through the breaking down of our own cultural barriers, as we came to grasp more of the whole sweep of world-history and to extend the modern flight network over distant regions of the globe. But even now, with this new appreciation there is bound up the illusion that modern technique itself has united these oases into a single world-culture. The fact is that technology has brought to an end everywhere the hitherto existing patterns of culture and imposed a "secondary system" in the form of a massive network, which must be regarded as quite as desolate and inhospitable as the world of primitive nature. On all sides today, therefore, there is an urgent need of legal guarantees of a worthy human existence. The law, of course, cannot do more than this: to bring into existence and to foster cultural forms is beyond its power, a task which again in the new conditions may take the form of pioneer work in oases.

Precisely because of the super-dimensional character of the general situation, all personal achievement of this kind is compelled to start out from small beginnings and to prove itself on a small scale. At this stage, the human task is perhaps exposed to the greatest danger through vanity and the craving to achieve only great things. In the past the desire for fame might well have been to a large extent a legitimate motive of action and planning; in the publicity of the "secondary system" it has lost most of its justification and can scarcely look beyond a certain prominence in organizing, cultural or sporting activity to the prospect of living on in history. We need indeed to ask ourselves how far the organized supply of publicity—for instance, a political event on the cinema screen—has again raised doubts about the character of public life, a question hotly debated in the nineteenth century. In any event, it seems today that if personal and objective relationships are to be taken seriously, there must be an absolutely free and close contact, screened off from the outer world: the world at large being excluded to a considerable extent even from the knowledge of this and absolutely excluded from passing judgment.

If we take seriously in this sense what may well be presented by modern publicity as a merely private affair, then there is no excuse for the habit of confusing liberty with arbitrary choice. The liberty of the person is in fact restricted by both the objects and the individuals with which he has to deal. He is not free to do simply what he wants, nor even what is permissible. We have already spoken of the idea that whatever is lawful may in fact be done as a serious flaw in Christian morality as hitherto understood: we must again clearly recognise that continual blunders within the field of what is morally permissible are as much a fault on the part of the human person and, for the people and things with which he is involved, just as fatal and destructive as infringements of the moral law. Here lies, incidentally, the point at which the sphere of what the theologians call the "natural" (as distinct from the supernatural) loses its merely formal character as an "occasion" and acquires an indispensable and constitutive importance for morality and religion, since any constructive effort for "edification" (as distinct from arbitrary choice within the field of the permissible) can succeed only in the right association with the right things.

This fundamental importance precisely of "secular" conduct cannot be suppressed by invoking the familiar theological notions of the transitory or secondary character of things. It must be made clear that our whole life—including our sacramental life—goes on precisely in this transitory world and that it is a failure unless the possibilities of the present time—again including the sacramental sphere—are positively grasped. Such a positive approach, however, requires the exclusion of whatever is impossible in the actual situation, even though in itself and from the moral standpoint it is permissible. In a responsible association with objects and with competent persons, the appreciation of such requirements may be practised and its fulfilment tested. The final orientation and transcendent responsibility must of course be left to the conscience of the individual, which by rising above the dark sense of guilt and the labyrinth of casuistry can develop in this field its creative function.

Notes

CHAPTER I

[1] This factor appears to have been neglected even at the great international congress of historians in Mainz in 1955, devoted to the theme: "Europe, Heritage and Mission." See vol. 13 of the publications of the Institute of European History, Universal History Division, Mainz, edited by M. Göhring, Wiesbaden, 1956.

[2] Cf. B. Welte, "Wahrheit und Geschichtlichkeit" in *Saeculum* 3, 1952, pp. 177-91.

[3] A decisive debate in 1519 between Eck (professor of theology at Ingolstadt) and Carlstadt, a follower of Luther (Tr.).

[4] Henri de Lubac, S.J., *Catholicism* (English translation by Lancelot C. Sheppard), London, 1950, p. 202.

[5] This clearly holds also for English Catholicism (Tr.).

CHAPTER II

[1] Cf. B. Spuler, "Islamische und abendländische Geschichtsschreibung", in *Saeculum*, vol. 6, 1955, p. 132.

[2] The problem is clearly stated by W. Kamlah, *Christentum und Geschichtlichkeit*, Stuttgart, 1951, pp. 99f.

[3] See my article, "Philosophie, Geschichte und Katholizität" in *Philos. Jahrb. der Görresgesellschaft*, vol. 68, 1960, pp. 279-89.

[4] *Phänomenologie des Geistes*, VI, B, III: "Die absolute Freiheit und der Schrecken". In J. B. Baillie's translation (*The Phenomenology of Mind*, London, 1931, p. 598), the title of this section is "Absolute Freedom and Terror" and a footnote explains that the term "terror . . . refers primarily to the regime under the French revolutionaries" (Tr.).

CHAPTER III

[1] M. Pohlenz, *Die Stoa*, Göttingen, 1948, vol. I, pp. 198, 262. Also E. Voegelin, *Order and History*, vol. II ("The World of the Polis"), Louisiana, State University Press, 1957, p. 13.

[2] M. Pohlenz, *op. cit.*, vol. I, p. 157.

[3] M. Pohlenz, *op. cit.*, vol. I, p. 336.

[4] *Anal. post.* 99b-100a. Translation by G. R. G. Mure in *The Works of Aristotle* translated into English under the editorship of W. D. Ross, vol. I, Oxford, 1926.

[5] E. Topitsch, *Vom Ursprung und Ende der Metaphysik*, Vienna, 1958.

[6] H. Leisegang, *Denkformen*, Berlin, 1951², p. 450.

[7] E. Topitsch, *op. cit.*, pp. 137f.

[8] E. Topitsch, *op. cit.*, pp. 122, 180; A. Dempf, *Kritik der historischen Vernunft*, Vienna, 1957, p. 156.

[9] A. Dempf, *Weltordnung und Heilsgeschichte*, Einsiedeln, 1958, p. 122.

[10] E.g., *Phys.* II, 194b; *Metaph.* 1059a, 1072b.

[11] *Metaph.* 1073a.

[12] On the Christian acceptance of this view cf. M. Pohlenz, *op. cit.*, vol. I, pp. 411, 416, 427.

[13] A. Dempf, *Kritik*, pp. 146, 166f.

[14] London, 1924, *passim*, especially pp. 308f. Penguin Ed., 1955, pp. 334f.

[15] Cf. also P. E. Schramm, *Herrschaftszeichen und Staatssymbolik, Beiträge zu ihrer Geschichte vom 3. bis zum 16. Jahrhundert*, 3 vols. Stuttgart, 1954-56, p. 1087, on Rabanus' elaboration of the Etymologies of Isidore of Seville.

[16] A. Jungmann, S.J., *Missarum Solemnia*, Freiburg, 1952, vol. I, pp. 114-20, 143-6. English translation by Francis A. Brunner, C.SS.R., revised by C. K. Riepe, *The Mass of the Roman Rite: its origin and development*, London 1959 (abridged edition), pp. 66-9, 81-9.

[17] It is important to note that a mere translation of the Latin does not help much in the understanding of the liturgy, least of all if it aims at edification and only succeeds in concealing the meaning of the texts. What most needs to be done is to develop the mother tongue as a sacral language out of the resources of both religious and linguistic experience.

[18] Jungmann, *op. cit.*, p. 155; English trans., p. 88.

CHAPTER IV

"Nec ipsos majores nostros ad fidei vestrae confessionem tam ratione ductos quam vi victos crederemus, sicut et vestrae consentiunt historiae. Ante imperatorum quippe vel principum ad fidem vestram per miracula, ut dicitur conversionem, paucos sapientum vel nullos vestra purificatio acquisivit, quamvis tum facile a patentissimis idolatriae erroribus gentes possent evelli et in quemcumque unius Dei cultum transferri." *Dialogus inter philosophum judaeum et christianum*, P.L., 178, col. 1658 BC.

[2] Jungmann, *op. cit.*, I, pp. 414f; Eng. trans., pp. 213f.

[3] Luke 10.3.

[4] J. Voigt, *Constantin d.Gr. und sein Jahrhundert*, Munich, 1949, esp. pp. 192ff. and 244f.; A. Kaniuth, *Die Beisetzung Konstantins d.Gr.*, Breslau, 1941 (with bibliography).

[5] J. Buchkremer, *Dom zu Aachen, Beiträge zur Baugeschichte* II, *Vom Königstuhl und seiner Umgebung*, Aachen, 1941, p. 38 and illustration 7 on p. 34. The symbolic expression of early times is evident in itself without being corroborated by discursive thinking—which had not then been developed. It would therefore be futile to look for literary meanings in the direct speech of the symbol.

[6] A. Michel, "Der Kaiser und die Kirche", in *Ostkirchliche Studien* 2 (1953), 3 (1954), 4 (1955) and 5 (1956); H. G. Beck, *Kirche und theologische Literatur im byzantinischen Reich*, Munich, 1959, pp. 1 and 36f.

[7] M. Grabmann, *Geschichte der katholischen Theologie*, Darmstadt, 1956, vol. II, pp. 194f. (In English a note on the subject will be found in F. Cayré,

Manual of Patrology, translated by H. Howitt, Tournai, 1940, vol. II, p. 419, n.I.—Tr.)

[8] Jungmann, *op. cit.*, I, p. 156, n. 90; Eng. trans., p. 89. We may observe also the cautious way in which even today Yves Congar had to draw attention to the need of appreciating the importance of the humanity of Christ: see *Christ, Our Lady and the Church*, translated by Henry St John, London, New York, Toronto, 1957, pp. 45f.

[9] E. Ewig, "Zum christlichen Königsgedanken im Frühmittelalter" in *Das Königtum. Seine geistigen und rechtlichen Grundlagen*, Lindau and Constance, 1956, p. 31.

[10] *Ibid.*, p. 22; cf. MGH Ep. III, 457-60.

[11] E. Ewig, *art. cit.*, pp. 57f. and 73.

[12] A. Michel, *art. cit.* in *Ostkirchliche Studien* 5 (1956), p. 30.

CHAPTER V

[1] The term *Wurt* eventually gave way to the vaguer expression, *Schicksal*. This development is regarded by Hauck as the sign of a new epoch (A. Hauck, *Kirchengeschichte Deutschlands*, 1952, vol. II, p. 756. On faith in miracles and the cult of relics, see p. 181).

[2] The best account of this is found in H. de Boor, "Germanische und christliche Religiosität" in *Mitteilungen der schlesischen Gesellschaft für Landeskunde*, xxxiii (1933), pp. 26-52.

[3] Quoted by Spengler, *Decline of the West*, English translation by Charles F. Atkinson, London, 1934, vol. II, p. 277.

[4] Jacobus de Voragine, *Legenda Aurea*. English translation, *The Golden Legend*, by William Caxton, edited by F. S. Ellis, London, 1900, vol. VI, p. 157.

[5] F. L. Ganshof, *La Belgique carolingienne*, Brussels, 1958, p. 130; on the cult of relics, see p. 141: "il y avait là une 'matérialisation' de la piété chrétienne, bien proche de la superstition."

[6] Cf. Bernhard Toepfer, "Reliquienkult und Pilgerbewegung zur Zeit der Klosterreform im burgundisch-aquitanischen Gebiet" in *Vom Altertum zum Mittelalter* (*Festschrift* for H. Sproemberg), p. 420.

[7] For Cluny's practice cf. G. Schreiber, *Gesammelte Abhandlungen* I, *Gemeinschaften des Mittelalters. Recht und Verfassung, Kult und Frömmigkeit*, pp. 81-150; also G. Tellenbach (Editor), *Neue Forschungen über Cluny und die Cluniazenser*, Freiburg, 1959.

[8] H. J. Rothemund, *Ikonenkunst*, Munich, 1954, pp. 9 and 58. E. Benz, *Geist und Leben der Ostkirche*, Hamburg RDE 40 (1957), p. 11. Benz rightly begins his interpretation of the spirit of the Eastern Church with a chapter on icons.

[9] Already at the time of the Iconoclast conflict the argument was occasionally adopted that the Eucharist, being consubstantial, was the only true image. Cf. H. G. Beck, *Kirche und theologische Literatur im byzantinischen Reich*, Munich, 1959, p. 302.

[10] P. Browe, S.J., *Die Verehrung der Eucharistie im Mittelalter*, Munich, 1933, p. 89. It was also the custom, if there were no relics available, to place one or two hosts in the altar. Cf. J. Braun, *Der christliche Altar in seiner geschichtlichen Entwicklung*, Munich, 1924, vol. I, p. 544.

[11] Jungmann, *op. cit.*, I, p. 279; English translation, p. 156.

[12] T. Zwölfer, *Sankt Peter. Apostelfürst und Himmelspförtner. Seine Verehrung bei den Angelsachsen und Franken*, Stuttgart, 1929.

[13] P. Browe, S.J., *op. cit.*, p. 90.

[14] Cf. F. Dölger, "Rom in der Gedankenwelt der Byzantiner" in *Zeitschrift für Kirchengeschichte*, vol. LVI (1937), pp. 39f.

[15] P. E. Schramm, *Herrschaftszeichen und Staatssymbolik*, Stuttgart, 1954-56, pp. 312, 340, 994, 1098.

[16] c.24: "Quod non sunt coequande imagines reliquiis sanctorum martyrum et confessorum . . . eo quod reliquie aut de corpore sunt aut de his, quae circa corpus cuiusdam sancti fuerunt, imagines vero nec in corpore nec circa corpus fuisse vel fore creduntur illis, quibus adscribunter." MGH. Leg. III. T. 2 suppl., p. 153. Cf. also p. 138 (c. 16): "Restat, ut nos sanctos in eorum corporibus vel potius reliquiis corporum seu etiam vestimentis veneremur juxta antiquorum patrum traditionem (!), illi vero parietes et tabulas adorantes (!) in eo se arbitrentur magnum habere fidei emolumentum, ei quod operibus sint subjecti pictorum."

[17] *Corpus Mysticum: L'Eucharistie et l'Eglise au moyen-âge*, Paris, 1949².

[18] This transformation of faith is noted also by A. Dempf, *Die unsichtbare Bilderwelt*, Einsiedeln, 1959, pp. 234f., but he ascribes it wholly to the influence of the Germanic spirit on the Roman world.

[19] P. Browe, S.J., "Die eucharistischen Wunder des Mittelalters" in *Studien zur historischen Theologie* NF 4, Breslau, 1938; cf. also the same author's *Die Verehrung der Eucharistie im Mittelalter*, Munich, 1933.

[20] H. de Lubac, S.J., *op. cit.*, p. 269. "Fides quaerens intellectum" is no longer faith growing in understanding, but simply seeking a rational defence (Tr.).

[21] This was developed by theology about 1150, defined as dogma at the Council of Lyons in 1274.

[22] See n. 8, chap. IV.

CHAPTER VI

[1] E. Ewig, "Zum christlichen Königsgedanken im Frühmittelalter" in *Das Königtum: Seine geistigen und rechtlichen Grundlagen*, Lindau and Constance, 1956, p. 37.

[2] The influence in itself was a legacy from the monasticism of St Basil, which found expression in the West in the form of Celtic monasticism. Even at the time of St Basil monastic ethics had come to be regarded as ethics absolutely speaking. Cf. D. Amand, *L'ascèse monastique de St Basile*, Maredsous, 1945, pp. 12 and 28f.; H. G. Beck, *Kirche und theologische Literatur im byzantinischen Reich*, Munich, 1959, p. 90.

[3] "Nam haec, Deo gratias, a temporibus Vitaliani papae, et Theodori Dorobernensis Archiepiscopi inolevit in ecclesia Anglorum consuetudo, et quasi legitima tenebatur, ut non solum clerici in monasteriis, sed etiam laici cum conjugibus et familiis suis ad confessores suos pervenirent, et se fletibus et carnalis concupiscentiae consortio his duodecim diebus cum elemosinarum largitione mundarent, quatenus puriores Dominicae communionis perceptionem in Natale Domini perciperent." *Dialogus Egberti* (c. 750) quoted by Oscar D. Watkins, *A History of Penance*, London and New York, 1920, p. 636.

[4] ". . . tribunal enim Christi altare, et corpus suum inibi cum sanguine judicat indignos accedentes". *Poenitentiale Columbani* c. 30, apud Watkins, p. 595.

[5] On the history of penance see B. Poschmann, *Die abendländische Kirchenbusse im Ausgang des christlichen Altertums*, Munich, 1928, and *Die abendländische Kirchenbusse im frühen Mittelalter*, Breslau, 1930; J. A. Jungmann, *Die lateinischen Bussriten in ihrer geschichtlichen Entwicklung*, Innsbruck, 1932; A. Mortimer, *The Origins of Private Penance in the Western Church*, Oxford, 1939; Paul Anciaux, *The Sacrament of Penance*, London, 1962; John M. T. Barton, *Penance and Absolution*, London, 1961 (Tr.); O. Teetaert, O.F.M.Cap., *La confession aux laïques dans l'Eglise latine depuis de 8e jusqu'au 14e siècle*, Louvain, 1949.

[6] *Ep.* 112, Migne, *P.L.* 100, col. 337. Alcuin also asserted that it was necessary to go to Confession before every reception of Holy Communion (*De Psalmorum Usu* ii, 9, *P.L.*, 101, col. 499). On Communion without previous Confession as a point of accusation in the *Confiteor* cf. Jungmann, *Bussriten*, p. 173.

[7] Quoted in *Merkur*, No. 140, 1959, p. 936.

[8] On the prohibition of usury see Max Weber, *Grundriss der Sozialökonomik*, Tübingen, 1925, pp. 801f.; Karl Mannheim, *Ideology and Utopia*, London, 1936, p. 85.

[9] Cf. A. Castro, *The Structure of Spanish History* (translated by Edward L. King), Princeton, 1954, p. 626.

[10] C. J. Jung, *Flying Saucers: A Modern Myth of Things Seen in the Sky*, English translation by R. F. C. Hull, London, 1959, p. 66.

[11] E. Michel, *Rettung und Erneuerung des personalen Lebens*, Frankfurt, 1951, p. 103.

[12] K. Sommermann, in *Merkur*, No. 134, 1959, p. 382.

[13] E. Rosenstock-Huessy, *Die europäischen Revolutionen und der Character der Nationen*, Stuttgart, 1951.

[14] Typical is the development of the Spirituals in the thirteenth century (see pp. 122ff.). Friedrich Heer gives an illuminating example in *Die dritte Kraft: Der europäische Humanismus zwischen den Fronten des konfessionalen Zeitalters*, Frankfurt, 1959, p. 97. We can see the mentality at work already among the higher clergy at the time of Louis the Pious. Led by Agobard of Lyons, the bishops attempted "without regard for the historical data and relying on the Bible alone, to establish the unity of the West under the rule of the Emperor in a single revolutionary charge" (H. Lowe, in *Rhein. Vierteljahrsbl.*, No. 17, 1950, p. 161).

[15] W. Kamlah, *Christentum und Geschichtlichkeit*, Stuttgart, 1951, p. 27.

[16] *Ibid.*, p. 294.

CHAPTER VII

[1] Américo Castro, *España en su historia: Cristianos, moros y judíos*; English translation by Edward L. King, *The Structure of Spanish History*, Princeton, 1954 (especially pp. 130f.). For the application of the idea to death purely in the service of politics, cf. E. H. Kantorowicz, *The King's Two Bodies*, Princeton, 1957, pp. 252f.

[2] Cf. H. J. Hüffer, "Die spanische Jakobusverehrung und ihre Ausstrahlungen auf Deutschland" in *Hist. Jahrb. der Görresges.* 74 (1958), pp. 124f.

[3] For the first time in the *Memoriale Sanctorum* of Eulogius of Seville (851); cf. A. Castro, *op. cit.*, p. 219. For its influence on the West cf. K. Heisig, "Geschichtsmetaphysik des Rolandsliedes" in *Zeitschrift für romanische Philologie* 55 (1935).

[4] The standard work of E. G. Grimme, *Aachener Goldschmiedekunst im Mittelalter von Karl d.Gr. bis zu Karl V.*, describes the event as a promise of James to give Charlemagne his "support", thus taking away from the picture any concrete meaning. That the reference to the Hohenstaufens was known is evident from a note of the *Annales Cameracenses* in 1159: in these the Emperor of "Galicia" appears on the same level as Barbarossa and the Byzantine Emperor (MGSS xvi, p. 532). Cf. also H. J. Hüffer, "Die mittelalterliche spanische Kaiseridee und ihre Probleme" in *Saeculum*, 3 (1952), pp. 428-443.

CHAPTER VIII

[1] P. E. Schramm, *Herrschaftszeichen und Staatssymbolik*, Stuttgart, 1954-56, pp. 69, 578f.

[2] H. Hoffmann, "Ivo von Chartres und die Lösung des Investiturstreits" in *Deutsches Archiv*, 15 (1959), esp. p. 417. On this theme see particularly G. Ladner, *Theologie und Politik vor dem Investiturstreit*, Baden-Vienna, 1938, and G. B. Borino (Ed.), *Studi Gregoriani*, vols. I-V, Rome, 1947-57.

[3] L. A. Veit, *Der Zusammenbruch des Mainzer Erzstuhls*, Mainz, 1927, pp. 46f. Under the influence of the ideas of the Enlightenment, the Prince-Archbishop forbade the Orders even to acquire real estate (*ibid.*, p. 52). Cf. also, on pp. 120f., the illuminating comments on property in "dead hands" before secularization. According to F. Lütge (*Die bayrische Grundherrschaft*, Stuttgart, 1949, p. 35) property of this kind in Bavaria before secularization amounted to 51 to 56% of the land.

[4] E. W. Kemp, *Canonization and Authority in the Western Church*, Oxford, 1948.

[5] Cf. Otto von Freising, *Chronica* VII, Hofmeister, p. 310: "Porro ecclesiam ecclesiasticas personas eorumque sectatores, tam ex usu locutionis quam considerationis potioris partis diximus."

[6] "Ideo est alius status ecclesiae nunc et tunc, non tamen est alia ecclesia" (*Quodlibet* xii, q. 13, a. 19). This illuminating observation is thrown out casually as an argument by Aquinas.

[7] G. Ladner, "The Concepts of 'Ecclesia' and 'Christendom' and their Relation to the Idea of Papal 'Plenitudo Potestatis' from Gregory VII to Boniface VIII" in *Sacerdotio e regno da Gregorio VII a Bonifacio VIII*. Rome, 1954. Cf. some pertinent comments in F. Kempf, S.J., *Papsttum und Kaisertum bei Innozenz III: Die geistigen und rechtlichen Grundlagen seiner Thronstreitspolitik*, Rome, 1954, p. 84.

[8] Kempf, *op. cit.*

[9] Art. 48 permitted the president to bring in the army to protect or restore public order, if this was seriously threatened or disturbed; in the same circumstances, he could suppress a number of constitutional liberties, including *habeas corpus*, freedom of speech and press, inviolability of home and property, secrecy of mail, telegraph and telephone, freedom of association; he was empowered to govern by emergency decrees; such measures and decrees had to be made known to the *Reichstag*, after they

had been taken, and they might then be rescinded. We all know what use Hitler made of these exceptional rights to gain and maintain power (Tr.).

[10] E. Ewig, "Zum christlichen Königsgedanken im Frühmittelalter" in *Das Königtum: Seine geistigen und rechtlichen Grundlagen*, Lindau and Constance, 1956, p. 31.

[11] P. E. Schramm, *op. cit.*, pp. 69, 578f.

[12] *Ibid.*, pp. 66f. Already in 1058 Nicholas II at his coronation, at the suggestion of Hildebrand (Gregory VII), put on a dual crown. Cf. J. Deér, *Schweizer Beiträge zur allgemeinen Geschichte* vii (1949), p. 54, and P. E. Schramm, in *Studi Gregoriani*, II, p. 443.

[13] Cf. C. Cahen, "L'idee de Croisade" in *Relazioni del X Congresso internazionale di Scienze storiche*, Rome, 1955, III, pp. 627f.

[14] N. Paulus, *Geschichte des Ablasses im Mittelalter vom Ursprung bis zur Mitte des 14. Jahrhunderts*, 3 vols., Paderborn, 1922-23.

[15] W. von den Steinen, *Der Kosmos des Mittelalters: Von Karl d.Gr. bis zu Bernhard von Clairvaux*, Berne-Munich, 1959, pp. 190f.; K. Erdmann, *Die Entstehung des Kreuzzugsgedankens*, reprint, Stuttgart, 1955. *Pataria* was the name given to a movement for Church reform in Milan in the tenth-eleventh centuries (Tr.).

[16] A. Castro, *The Structure of Spanish History*, Princeton, 1954, pp. 203f.

[17] E. Topitsch, *Vom Ursprung und Ende der Metaphysik*, Vienna, 1958.

[18] *Quodlibet*, XII, q. 13, a. 19.

[19] Cf. A. Dempf, *Kritik der historischen Vernunft*, Vienna, 1957, pp. 80, 190ff.

CHAPTER IX

[1] In spite of its marked sympathy for the Spirituals, the standard work on these events and the link between Francis and Joachim remains E. Benz, *Ecclesia Spiritualis, Kirchenidee und Geschichtstheologie der franziskanischen Reformation*, Stuttgart, 1934. A review of this book by the present writer appears in *Zeitschrift für Kirchengeschichte* 55 (1936) pp. 286f.

[2] K. Löwith, *Weltgeschichte und Heilsgeschehen*, Stuttgart, 1953. By demanding a distinction in principle between the concepts (world-history and salvation-event), Löwith renews on the historical plane the position of Berengarius of Tours and allows the problem to disappear.

[3] Cf. W. Stählin, *Die Gestalt des Antichristen und das Katechon*, in *Glaube und Geschichte, Festschrift* for J. Lortz, Baden-Baden, 1958, ii, pp. 1f.

[4] Cf. Karl Mannheim, *Diagnosis of Our Time*, London, 1943, p. 128: "Again there may be some who will feel that the real guarantee of the continuation of religious life is to be sought in the persistence of the much-despised conventions. Regular church-going and services, the observance of a certain ritual, orthodoxy on basic issues, are taken as a better guarantee of survival than those doubtful inner experiences of which you can never know where they will lead. This is a kind of religious behaviourism which existed long before behaviourism as a psychological doctrine. Just as the latter thinks that the creation of suitable habits is more important for the survival of the social order than highbrow ideas and doctrines, so this kind of ritualistic orthodoxy sees the guarantee of religion in the religious forms of habit-making."

CHAPTER X

[1] The first to observe that the social teaching of the Reformers was historically a step backwards, was Ernst Troeltsch (*The Social Teaching of the Christian Churches*, translated by Olive Wyon, London, 1931: original German edition, 1912). R. H. Tawney (*Religion and the Rise of Capitalism*, London, 1926) also shows very clearly how even the later emancipation of the Calvinist virtues towards a secularized economic outlook grew out of this unity of the Church and the world.

[2] On this subject see the shrewd observations of Denis de Rougement, *Man's Western Quest*, London, 1957, especially pp. 114f.

[3] In *Die Historisch-politischen Blätter*, VII (1841), pp. 178f., the claim is made that the Church is the axis on which everything turns and the real value of events must be judged in the light of their influence on the weal or woe of the Church. Politically, therefore, what serves the Church is good and what is opposed to her interests is bad. This point of view, typical of "political Catholicism", is a good example of the sociological misunderstanding of the Church and is only possible when her sacramental and mysterious character as the kingdom of God is projected into visible and earthly historical circumstances.

[4] Cf. n. 18, chap. VIII.

[5] Cf. A. Mirgeler, "Der Faschismus in der Geschichte des modernen Staates" in *Saeculum* VI (1950), p. 101.

[6] Cf. H. G. Beck, *Kirche und theologische Literatur im byzantinischen Reich*, Munich, 1959, p. 312.

[7] The Byzantine Emperor Leo VI declared the Church's blessing on marriage to be necessary by law. Until then the consent alone was legally necessary. Cf. H. G. Beck, *op. cit.*, p. 87. In the West the present-day practice in regard to marriage goes back, as we know, to the Council of Trent.

[8] The idea that this right of consultation belongs mainly or even exclusively to representatives of ecclesiastical organizations is an error arising from the sociological misunderstanding of the Church.